TABLE OF CONTE...

Notes for a Magazine 4
TAI FARNSWORTH
　Start with Woman 6
SAVANNAH SLONE
　We Dwelled Among Arches 7
SONNY PILLING
　She Had Brown Hair 10
LYNETTE YETTER
　A Feminist Love Poem 11
　Diving into the Wreck with Adrienne Rich 13
SHAWNTA SMITH-CRUZ
　Along the Boardwalk 15
　Dyke Hands and Dollar Vans 21
LAHL SARDYKE
　Prairie Blues 27
　This Thing Not Death 29
CAITLIN CROWLEY
　Empty 31
　Sister 32
LYNN MARTIN
　An Ordinary Window 33
KINNERY CHAPARREL
　loom. 39
　the wife of lot 42
EM SHEEHAN
　Am I? 44
MADARI PENDÀS
　Thirst 53
KAI COGGIN
　Chances Are 56

MICHELLE E. BROWN
  Who Will Know 62
SIERRA SCHWEITZER
  Love of my Youth 1 64
  Love of My Youth 2 65
LEE LYNCH
  The Gold Room 66
HANNAH LARRABEE
  We Were a Room 78
  Painter 80
KELSEY AHLMARK
  For Another Hundred Miles 81
S. b. SOWBEL
  Perspective 92
  Snowmelt 94
  Far From the Hive 96
NORA BECK
  Mother 97
TIMEA GULISIO
  The Buggy Ones 98
PATTY WILLIS
  Emergency Room in the Desert 103
  Psalm at Finisterre 106
  Psalm at a Time of Morning 109
SARAH YASUDA
  Coward Being 112
DEBORAH MIRANDA
  Fever 119
  Albuquerque 124
  Things Fire Can't Destroy 125
  Venice Beach 127
  Offerings 128
ANASTAZIA SCHMID
  The Tide 129

SARA KOPPEL
  Crescent Water 130
MEGHAN BELL
  Mary and the Mermaid 131
MARIPOSA
  Where Did Our Love Go 136
JADE HOMA
  Purgatory 144
BEC EHLERS
  Pillow Talk 145

  Book Reviews 147
  Contributors 161
  Sharing Our Lesbian Herstory 171
  Thank You to Volunteers, Interns, and Booksellers 174
  Advertisements 175

NOTES FOR A MAGAZINE

I'm writing this Notes for a Magazine while listening to Dr. Christine Blasey Ford testify in front of the Senate Judiciary Committee. It is early in the hearing; Dr. Ford just finished testifying. Senator Feinstein has just entered into the record one hundred, sixty letters supporting Dr. Ford from neighbors and over 1,000 letters from women physicians. The fact of these letters captures my imagination, and nearly reduces me to tears. These letters strike me as both congressional testimony and letters to the future, expressing perhaps promise or hope by women for a better future for all women. My hope listening to this hearing is that it is the last hearing needed for a Supreme Court nominee accused of misogynistic behavior. My fear is it will not be the last. Those letters, they contain the secret whispers of the future for how women will continue to speak out and resist.

In some ways, *Sinister Wisdom* is like those letters entered by Senators as testimony. The issues of *Sinister Wisdom* offer testimony of lesbian lives today; they also are a whisper and a promise to a future when lesbians are interested in reading the stories from these pages.

Sinister Wisdom 111: *Golden Mermaids* features some of the best work from lesbian writers and artists working today. It was a pleasure to assemble this issue with *Sinister Wisdom* intern, Sophia Moore. All of the work had been selected for the issue and Sophia helped me weave it together in the tapestry of this issue. I hope you love it as much as we both do.

Three other important items to share with you, our beloved readers and supporters. First, we continue to mail back issues from our "vault" as I have begun calling the 6,000 copies of back issues of *Sinister Wisdom* that are stored in my office. You may recall, I moved over 10,000 copies of back issues from a storage facility in Berkeley, California two years ago. We now have distributed about 5,000 copies of those issues into hands of readers all over the United States and around the world. That work continues. Every month or so, we select a new back issue from the "vault" to mail out with every package that leaves *Sinister Wisdom* for the month. We continue to donate copies of all available back issues to community centers, libraries, schools, prisons, and other places where lesbian readers can find and enjoy these books. This work will continue until we have fewer than 2,000 issues of the journal on hand. If you know somewhere we should send copies, please be in touch. Storing some back issues is an important function of *Sinister Wisdom*; we are dedicated to retaining our herstory. At the same time, the number of back issues stored needs to be manageable and not require a massive storage facility.

Second, *Sinister Wisdom* continues to be an institution that says yes to lesbians. *Sinister Wisdom* brought into print the letters of Audre Lorde and Pat Parker, saying yes to an important research project of mine. *Sinister Wisdom* published a 2019 calendar saying yes to the vision and labor of another intern, Sara Gregory, who created an amazing calendar that celebrates the herstory of *Sinister Wisdom* and looks forward to our future. What will *Sinister Wisdom* say yes to in the future? Bring us your wild ideas and imaginings! And join *Sinister Wisdom* in saying yes to lesbians any time you can.

Third, thank you for your support, financially and communally. I write these notes prior to even launching our fall fundraiser, but I know *Sinister Wisdom* will have the fall fundraiser, and I know that the amazing lesbians of the world will support the journal, and I want to thank them—and you—for your support. Thank you.

It is a pleasure to edit and publish *Sinister Wisdom*. I hope you enjoy reading *Sinister Wisdom* as much as I enjoy working on it. Thank you for making this work possible and for lifting it up in every way that you can.

In sisterhood,
Julie R. Enszer
January 2019

START WITH WOMAN

Tai Farnsworth

Start with a tree standing tall, roots pushing into resistant earth. Roots persisting, unyielding. Roots holding strong, not letting go, roots bursting through the sidewalk. Start with a stream. No, a river, a rush of water, turning rocks into sand. A river wearing away its edges. A river sometimes sweet and meandering, sometimes deadly. Start with wind. Wind rustling hair and cooling sweat on backs. Wind both soft and hard, giving and taking. Wind to bring flowers and wind to rip houses from their foundations, tear at the sky. Start with a flame. Fire from love. Human fire made with crushed mouths and desperate tongues. Fire that rarely burns but always can. Start with the ocean. Salty, warm, wet. Ocean for cradling bodies, rocking them to sleep, holding them close. Ocean for pounding and sweeping away. Ocean to create and ocean to destroy. Start with the sun. Hot and unforgiving. The sun to bring warmth, the sun to set everything ablaze. Sun to kiss, for eternity. Start with the moon. Full and bright. Sitting in the sky like a promise. Sometimes a grin, sometimes a perfect O. Tempting an orgasm. Start with brilliance, and kindness, and fury, and rage. Start with yes and no and maybe. Start with bitch and cunt, goddess and queen, more and more and more. Start with you. Start with me. Start with us. Start with woman. Start with Woman.

WE DWELLED AMONG ARCHES

Savannah Slone

I swerved through windy roads, hugged to feel small between canyons of red rock. My crinkled, printed out directions took me past sloping juniper trees that looked straight out of a Dalí painting. Boulders that could kill. Dusty lavender clouds a shadow to the neon hues of pink and blood orange. Shallow creeks that mirrored the landscape beyond back into itself. Arches existed in layers. All reminders of our insignificance.

I pulled up, guardedly, to my new place of employment. A crisp Utah sunrise welcoming me.

Locking my Jeep door with two chirp-like clicks, I approached the entrance to the ranch. I knocked hard on the thick, oak door. An older man, maybe mid-50s, let me in. He adorned his timeworn body in Levi's, old boots, and a button up plaid shirt.

"It's Ms. Anson, right?" He held a manila folder in his calloused hands.

"Yes, sir."

"And you're from Texas?"

"Yep. San Antonio."

"Well, Ms. Anson from San Antonio. You ever been to Anson?" He offered a grin.

"I actually haven't, believe it or not. That's near Abilene, yeah?"

"Yes, ma'am, right near there. That's where my daddy grew up. I spent my summers, as a kid, down there." His dense, white mustache hid his upper lip.

Our small talk continued, as he showed me to my room. His name was Quentin, but I could call him Q. He left me to settle in. Room and board made up the majority of my pay. The room felt very vacation cabin-y. There was a reclaimed wood headboard with a matching nightstand and dresser, all stained the same shade of red cedar. The linens were forest green. A skylight directly above the bed hinted at my impending days of early rising. I began to unpack my yellow duffel bag, when a low knock indicated Q's reappearance at my door.

"Hey, Anson, it's me again," sounded his husky voice.

I opened it up and he stood with a tall woman, dressed much like himself.

"This is Ley Jonz. You'll be working directly with her a lot more than me, so she'll be showing you around the property whenever you're ready."

"Lee Jones? As in Tommy Lee Jones?"

"No, ma'am. Ley is short for Wheatley and Jonz is spelled J-O-N-Z." She had a seductive way of spelling out her own name—her voice thick, raw honey.

I smiled a likely dopey smile.

"Ley is my niece," said Q. "I told her all about how you're from Texas and ain't ever been to Anson, even with that last name of yours."

We giggled obligatorily and I closed my door. I walked along side her. She walked with her dark, delicate hands tucked into the pockets of her high-waisted jeans. I found myself caught up in Brokeback Mountain fantasies. Pushing my hips against hers, up against an arching canyon. Rattlers entangling themselves around our interwoven legs. My hands caressing her breasts. Spiders and scorpions would crawl up my ankles, but I wouldn't mind. To die with my lips on hers would be just fine. But my fantasies were probably just that—fantasy.

I was a short, chubby butch girl. If she fed into appearance stereotypes, she surely assumed I was a dyke. She wouldn't be wrong, but I still hated that it was assumed because I didn't have long flowing hair or wore frilly dresses. However, I seemed to have been born without any sort of gaydar and was simultaneously unaware of when girls, in the past, were digging me.

We were the only ladies on the ranch. Ley and I spent a lot of time together. She invited me to do things with her. We went river rafting, hiking, climbing, and biking. We sighed at the busyness and increasing prices in town, thanks to the tourists. Ley taught me about the different flora and fauna of the area. I was able to identify different types of hawks and eagles. I spotted a black-billed magpie and a sage sparrow. I differentiated between Mormon tea and cliffrose shrubs. I taught her how to play the ukulele. I read her poems I had written, though not the ones about her. We sat in lawn chairs and drank beer, as swarms of bats erupted each evening. Right at dusk, one night, she casually mentioned an ex-girlfriend of hers. During that same sunset, we shared our first kiss. I let her initiate it and later found out that she had been waiting for me to make the first move.

She and I brushed our caramelized brown horses and their black manes. We worshipped them and their dusty shoes and their Western wear. We led them by their bridles, as they hauled wealthy white children and their wealthy white mothers. We exchanged unspoken flirtations and tense smirks. It got us through our scorching workdays. Ley, my nocturnal goddess, would sneak into my room, after Q and the boys were snoring. Moonlight from the skylight overhead illuminated her small breasts. We melted into one another every night. She would fade into the shadows and resurface at dawn, exhausted but never showing it.

At the end of the summer, Ley went back to school. I was to head off on my next escapade, but I was welcome to return the following work season. My time in Moab was merely an anecdote in the vast fable of the universe. Yet still, I cherished every breath taken and landscape witnessed, alongside that companionable soul, as if it were the start and end to the entirety of my days.

SHE HAD BROWN HAIR

Sonny Pilling

She had brown hair that curled around
Her ears/ We hulled strawberries in/
Her mother's kitchen/ up to our elbows
In cold water/ Sunlight on her shoulder/
She said *I didn't tell him no/* She said *I just
Kind of froze/* She said *I just kind of let
It happen/* She said *it was my first time/*
I wanted to kiss her shoulder/ I wanted
To wring his neck/ To make a scene/ The
Strawberries bobbed like severed heads/
In cold water/

A FEMINIST LOVE POEM

Lynette Yetter

Writing a love poem
I do not write about your lips
nor your eyes,
nor your body.
Yet all that is you lives in this container.
Walks on your strong legs
with stubby feet and toes
whose nails are difficult to cut because
the creative way they grow.

Your creativity
your soul and huge heart
who always look for
ways to
help people.

"Do you need help? Support? Take your garbage to the dump?"
You offer.
"You see, I have my blue Toyota truck
who has traveled more thousands of miles than
the astronauts flew to the moon.
I have my leather gloves,
that maintain the form of my working hands.
Another skin to me
when I yank weeds from the dry and hard land,
when I split wood,
when I help you remove trash from your basement,
from your garage,
from your dead friend's room -
the clothes of her bed dyed and encrusted with life's fluids

from her ultimate moments before going to the hospital
for the last time."

What strength you have.
You and I.
There is no separation in my words.
We are a strong couple,
in love and kindness.

No. I will not write about your lips.
But I love you with all my heart.
I feel I'm the luckiest woman in the world to find you
and dress my hands with leather gloves
in the form of your working hands
together we lift the things of life
together we enjoy the creations of the other.

I admire your creations.
Happiness stations that you invented for our cat.
The cat who does not go outside because she is old.
The cat eats green grass growing
on the shelf next to her folded blanket
in the window where
she watches birds eating
seeds you gave them.

So much happiness grows and flows because of you.

I love you I love you
I love you I love you.
That's how it is.

DIVING INTO THE WRECK WITH ADRIENNE RICH

Lynette Yetter

Diving into the wreck with Adrienne Rich, I prepare by watching YouTube. (To refresh my memory of her reference to Cousteau. His all-male world under the sea, on land, and in his boat, Calypso.) "Aye, Calypso" John Denver sings a love song to Jacques Cousteau—a manly man who says things such as "The sea is the mother of us all" and "I am the sea and the sea is me". Sounds like earth-based feminist spirituality to me! John sings "to live on the land we must learn from the sea. To be true as the tide and free as a wind swell, joyful and loving in letting it be." Now these John and Jacques examples of masculinity I celebrate. Full humanity. But where are the women? Adrienne and I strap on our scuba gear and rubber flippers and dive into the sunken wreck of globalized patriarchy; she carries the book of myths, her camera and sharp knife.

She went their first,
alone.
The only one.
To remind us that we are all one.
Fully human.
Celebrating our full humanity, we lesbians,
we females
whose names were ignored, marginalized, erased
in the patriarchal writing of the book of myths.

Diving into the wreck with Adrienne Rich, our powerful thigh muscles kick

the long rubber flippers
we swim unflappable

depths of Mother Sea's womb
where the wreck rots into food.

We celebrate, Adrienne Rich and I, our embodied full humanity. As Jacques Cousteau embodied his full humanity with his boat Calypso and spoken love of our Mother the sea. And John Denver embodied his full humanity singing his love of the men on the Calypso, his love and respect of Mother Nature as teacher and guide as he smiles from his Essentials album cover with his shaggy hair and flowered shirt. Under the sea by the wreck, bubbles of oxygen rising from her strapped-on scuba gear,

Adrienne writes her name in the book of myths.

She passes the book of myths to me
to pass to you
as we all and each tell our stories—celebrating
embodying our full humanity
just the way we are.

ALONG THE BOARDWALK

Shawnta Smith-Cruz

[A couple of old friends meet on a boardwalk for a rekindling.]

- Old friend, it is good to see you.
[a hug]
- As it is you.

[a smile. They walk, overlooking the ocean.]

- I have recently decided that I want to be skinny. Not because of the fashion of it, nor the feminist ideal of reclamation of the perceived beauty of a lesbian body. But because it was in the examining of a faceless body standing before me in perfect alignment and stature, that I came to the notion in my mind. Somehow, this woman...
- Faceless, you say?
- Well, not exactly faceless. But just that, her face does not matter to the story.
- Is this a story? Let's sit.

[they sit. On a bench, overlooking the ocean]

- It is more a revelation than a story; will you listen?
- I am listening.
- It is about her jeans.
- Her genes?
- No, not her genes, but her jeans, or rather, not her jeans but her legs, or how her jeans stood with her legs, instead of on top of them, her legs being inside. Something about her legs, or her jeans, made me aware of both her jeans and her legs, as separate entities.

[a bird flies overhead and a droplet of bird shit falls on the space between them, causing a brief pause and shuffle]

I immediately assumed that she had to be wearing heels in order to balance her upheld shoulders... Her back was turned to me. Let me start over.
- Okay, you may. Please begin again.
- I'm at the library, in deep contemplation, as one is often when inside a library. There is silence, large windows, a sunny disposition and day surrounded me. As I moved about the space, I couldn't help but notice the change of the clouds, and so began to glance outside the window, up from my book, for a prolonged period of time. It looked like rain, and so, some of the people walking outside hovered against the building to shield themselves, I presume, from the surprise approaching storm. Of the few that chose the wall of windows as shelter, one was a woman. Others may have been women as well, but one in particular, she stole my gaze from the clouds and the entire scene, until all that I could see were her legs. Her jeans, and her legs, and if I were to move my glance upward her scapula, do you know, the winged bone at her back, was in perfect distance to the rim of her ass.
- You mean her buttocks.
- That's what I said. Yes. Her ass was leaning against the metal bar outside of the building, but she leaned as far inward as she could, so there was in fact, a cushioning formed where the metal bar was cupped by the flesh, but really, by the jeans.
- The dungarees.
- Yes, precisely. The fabric was suddenly an incubator for her body on the corner of 34th street on a windy city afternoon. It was almost a travesty, that her body was held in such a way, confined. She moved forward and backward to watch for the sky and in such forward alignment, then backward, her arch resembled what I've seen only in Jordache jean commercials, allowing her ass to display

itself as if horizontal before me. I became transfixed. It wasn't until she began to turn sideways, her body in the direction of the wind, in the same direction as the passer-by tourists and office workers, did her pivot force me to notice that she was in fact not wearing heels. Instead, at the base of this statuesque rotation was slightly ashen, slightly wet feet comfortably mounted in Berkinstock sandals, flattened.
- No!
- Yes!
- Are you certain?
- Very certain!
- You mean to say that she wasn't wearing heels at all? But surely there was an arch inside of the sandal, some sort of incline that allowed the round formed section of her arse to supple its way affront your eyes, as she leaned in against that horizontal pole with its' cold metal giving her reason to protrude the bottom half of herself away from what stood before it: a dreadful, if not frightening canvas of grey autumn and lifelessness?
- I assure you. She was not wearing heels. My friend, instead, she was thin. She was elongated inside of her body, perfectly normal, nothing special, and I decided that I liked it. This was the tone of the silence that she stood in.
- Or perhaps that you stood in. Remember, you are the one who was inside of a library, while she was a character in a scene of fury on a greying city landscape.
- But that is it, not even a sigh came from her slim and magnificent body. Silence and posture only. A mannequin. When the rain began its descent in wisps, as if in the thickness of a cloud, the moisture that grabbed her attention was perhaps what led her little body to pressure its way back towards my notice. Likely, the way each raindrop, finally identifiable as more than a drop, less than a tear, speckling its incision onto the greyed streets, onto her face, painting then a gelled surface for the small amount of sunlight to absorb, creating a pattern atop her beige-colored

bowler jacket, illuminating the dimmed grey of the streets all but the small dry space that she'd created beneath her feet, and finally falling lightly atop the small, gripping, plump rounds of her blue dungarees, all of this made slim something holy and natural and free.

- And, so, we agree that there was then no need for heels.
- Yes, no need.
- But perhaps it was the rain, and not the woman at all.
- Why would you say this?
- The cleansing element of the water onto the land, perhaps this is what you were feeling after all. Perhaps you were in a rut of chemical association, the shifting of elements, the silence juxtaposed with the noise and premature bursting of the elements before you.
- No. I believe it was the woman and not the rain.
- Okay, fine. But why then has this image, this woman, this pair of legs, made you want to become thin? I would imagine it making you want to become timeless with no commitments, no bounds, no work to do, to run into, no life to consider having you constantly look to your watch or check your digital calendar, a kind of wanderlust with meditative qualities, but thinness? Explain.
- Simple. Although there was an alluring nature to her stance. I suddenly felt the myth of heterosexuality at its' best. I didn't want to push my groin against the creamy cushion of her backside, nor did I want to bend her back further to then stick my face between her dripping pinkness, while my hands wrapped themselves against her held hipbones, keeping her buckling steady. These intonations were not the first things that passed my mind. Instead, I was more intrigued at the sheer brilliance of her body. There was something clever to the arch. Without seeing her nude, I was assured that her nipples sat atop erect breasts, pointing northwards and watching the blackening sky. I wanted instead of pursing those nipples with my lips, to own a

pair of my own. For the first time in all of my dyke-ness, I wanted to be a part of the genius of her skin, so much that I wanted to be it, rather than simply knowing it, or claiming it, or appreciating it through her own knowing. Her slim figure made me realize the reason for her innocent yet alluring imposition. She had not a single unnecessary inch of skin. Every part of her center, her limbs, her angles, was useful.

- Oh, ode to the woman's body!

- Yes, the sleekness of a decaying corpse while alive is sensibly more attractive than an oily layered fat steamy blob...

- No, but I actually disagree with you, my friend. Your steamy blob of flesh, as you refer to the normal, is oily because it is meant to be rubbed without the rustic friction of dried passion. The decaying corpse of age, as you call it, is in essence the center of our souls and flesh merging into a rich combination of wisdom and depth. A woman who is narrow and precise fails to hold all that may come her way if in fact, her arms are outstretched and can only carry a burdened small load. I, for one, am often intrigued by what may be hidden between the contours of a woman's rolls, the crevice of the lines between heavy layers of fat, where my fingers could potentially find themselves, warmed and penetrating.

- But we speak of legs and ass, not arms and grip.

- Are the legs of a woman not an extension of her arms, each of them properly equipped to hold, grab, keep us within their grip?

- Why yes, but do you not prefer the wrapping of a pair of thin legs to seal you tightly, to find on the other end of their lock, a foot to encapsulate the ring, creating a lock, so that you may not loosen, so that you are held forever?

- Oh friend, not I. Freedom from grip is much more manageable from the embrace of arms, with connecting hands as a prize to the end. To rub and squeeze and placate my drifty nature is the essence of those hands, that grip of arms that I love will always let me go when I am ready.

[they stand]

- It seems we are too desirous of women's bodies to every truly want to become a woman's body other than our own, doesn't it?
- Indeed it does. And so too, it seems we may appreciate her beauty, and her body, while not losing sight of our own.

[they begin to walk]

- Agreed.

[a sigh. They continue to walk against the ocean, musing on the pinks and oranges of the sunset.]

DYKE HANDS AND DOLLAR VANS

Shawnta Smith-Cruz

Dyke hands.
Brooklyn Dyke hands.
Dollar Vans and Dyke hands.
There is something to be said for the feel of dyke hands.
Because dyke hands are the sexual organs of lesbian love.

I'm paying an ode to S. Diane Bogus who wrote a piece called Dyke Hands, first published in Common Lesbian Lives – A Lesbian Quarterly, No. 5 in the Fall of 1982. It became so popular that she published a book titled, *Dyke Hands & Sutras Erotic & Lyric* in 1988. I came across the 1982 version when sifting through the book shelf of an elder dykewoman. In her apartment during my house-sit, I thought that perhaps I could find a black dyke-womon inside of the pages of a journal created for dykes, not just women of color. And so I searched only with my fingers, not looking to the text, but feeling my way through the bookshelf of tattered edges, forgotten journals, archival ephemera, and stopped at the single out-dented seam that seemed thin enough to flip through as long as my attention would allow, and yet, central on the bookcase, curated not by a librarian, but by the hands of a dyke-womon publisher who would put her friends and favorites in the middle, to ensure they'd always be close to grab.

My dyke hands scrolled across the surface, and read the book jackets like brail, by the flecks of aged newsprint that fell to the side of the shelf as I continued to massage the spines detailing years of publication. Being born in 1983, the 1982 dyke year was perfect. The Fall of 1982 meant that I was soon to be, ruminating inside of my mother's womb, curating little fingers and nails in a dark wet space between her heart and her labia.

It was there that I found in Common Lesbian Lives, open to a middle article, and read aloud, Dyke Hands. Who cared about race when there were lesbians who wrote about sex? It wasn't until I got to the name of the narrator that I realized, it was indeed a black dyke womon, writing the word womon with two 'o's where the vowels live, that I knew the piece I had been searching for, the piece that my dyke hands led me to, was the right piece, at my fingertips, opening its pages to me, and eventually leading me to write the story of Peggy and Jan.

Peggy and Jan are seated inside of the cool movie theater.

It's Peggy's day off. She called Jan the night before, inviting her to a movie. It's the only thing they do together, cause Peggy works concessions at the theater, sometimes box office, but she prefers to be around the popcorn, and is really good at applying the right amount of butter, into the plastic-layered paper bag, shaking it, one additional scoop of popcorn, then just a tad more on top for dripping. Her manager keeps her there to train new staff. And although she ought to like the slight raise that being a trainer affords her, the additional $0.75 per hour is not the real reason she loves her job. It's the golden glow of the popcorn. It's the madness of explosive kernels volcanically emptying out of a metal-lidded enclave. Each time Peggy sees the head of the pot pop open, a piece of her purrs. It's the warm popcorn bag that she grips with her soft open dyke hands that keep her coming to concessions. The box office is filled with paper cuts. And Peggy, she doesn't use latex, so she needs to keep her fingers wholly uncut —safety first.

Jan doesn't even have a job, but is a student, on scholarship, with only enough money for her vices. Weed and beer with women, she'll spend her money on that.

"My hands are really warm. Sorry," Jan says while laying her palm over Peggy's, inside the darkness of the theater.

"Oh, no, it's okay. I'm kind of cold, so I like it." And Peggy does like it.

If we back track a little, it was fine for her that they were inside of her place of employment, cause it's what people did inside movie theaters; they sat close and touched each other. Dykes touched each other's dyke hands. They pressed knees together between scenes at the moments of film silence. They managed four-play inside of the popcorn bag, becoming warm and slippery and salty and ready to soon, after the movie, enter each other.

It's a proven fact, from an unknown source, that that's what dykes do in movie theaters. Over thirty years ago, S. Diane Bogus wrote that "Dyke Hands are the sexual organs of lesbian love..." So it goes with Dyke Hands... Now back to the story.

Peggy and Jan held hands in the dark.

Before Jan got to the movie theater, she knew she was running late. It was a cold night when Jan's dyke hands laced up her skippies, fingers fumbled with keys then locked her door and she ran against the wet pavement to the subway. The train said ten minutes before the next Manhattan bound, so instead of waiting, she headed upstairs to take a dollar van to Court Street movie theater. Her left arm held out her left dyke hand which flapped in the wind. Two honks came her way from a large green van. She got in. Jan squeezed beside an older woman whose hands clutched a bible, whose eyes stabbed at her, and in a single moment noticed Jan's baggy jeans, her upbent cap, and her protruding chest through her leather jacket. Jan's dyke hands stuffed headphones in her ears then began massaging the lint balls and copper coins in her pockets before any old-woman sermons could begin.

"Not today," she thought.

She found two-dollar bills when the van pulled off at green. Her eyes were averted to the window, and she slouched into the damp seclusion of the dollar van and her thoughts for how she could get to the theater, get to Peggy, place her reaching dyke hands against Peggy's cheek, grab the freckled skin, coddle her into a kiss.

When Jan was a girl, she'd take dollar vans on Church Avenue to Flatbush, living too far from the train to ever envision a walk to the most famous avenue that classified her hometown.

Dollar Vans were known for three things: their cheap fares, loud reggae music vibrating the seats, and the radio telecom where Driver would communicate if cops were near. They worked in threes, these cars: Flatbush, Utica, and Church. They went from $1 fare, to incremental fare shifts by quarter dollar, to now, twenty years later, a $2 flat rate. The worst thing you could do was not have exact change. And even worse than that, if you had a twenty-dollar bill, then you'd best let Driver know when you enter, that eventually, you're going to need change. And you'd best yell out your stop at least three to four blocks ahead, depending on the speed. Jan knew the rules. She also knew that Dollar Vans were known for a fourth thing, abrasive hands.

She needed the van to the last stop. Her favorite part was the approach to Eastern Parkway, always overcome by the grandeur of the Brooklyn Public Library's facade at Grand Army Plaza. Especially after it was recently renovated, the sun was glistening just so atop it's bronze-plated ornamental exterior. The smooth force of the van down the tree-lined haze of Flatbush avenue, the second hand residue of ganja in her nostrils, the sound of Beres Hammond's Sweetness sounding like soft brown skin against her tongue in candlelight, it was like a lover's grasp – she was in it, and on her way to Court street, the theater, and Peggy's touch.

She noticed the approach to Empire Blvd, the block before her beloved botanical garden view, when the van's music switched to dance hall, and the doors opened, the side man, screaming "Empire, last stop, Empire!" She needed to go to Court street, ten minutes north. She was the closest to the door, in the second seat, all the way to the left of the van, beside the tinted mildew window. "Court Street!!" she belted while her hands grabbed her bag. She angled her hat as she started to rise. "Excuse me, excuse, gettin' off..." other people said, pushing past her. She used her best patois, as other asses smacked her face. Annoyed riders kissed their teeth at her, were soured by the sudden announcement.

Their disrupted phone conversations, made hands clutch phones, slam onto seats. The entire van filled with women, young and old, kissed their teeth and sneered.

"Come, na chil, you na tink me naw afa go a wurk!" was directed at Jan, from the old woman whose bible looked like a stone in her palms. Jan began to rise when another woman took her hand and grabbed Jan's leg, very close to her inner thigh with her fingers, "Ouch" Jan grumbled. "You forgot uno hat," the young woman said with a smirk, blushing as Jan's hands crunched the top of her head, surprised that her short locks pricked her palm, embarrassed that her side-shaved haircut was exposed. The woman handed Jan her hat, playing a small tug a war with the brim. Jan didn't want to penetrate, to wrinkle her hat's rim, so she didn't pull back, just waited. Did this woman think that flirting was going to happen just because they were in an enclosed space? Was she not going to hand her her hat?

S. Diane Bogus considers the crime of when a lover's hand is offered to other women thoughtlessly for handshakes.

Knowing that Peggy would want popcorn, even though she worked there, it was a gesture of kindness for Jan to buy the bag. That meant she only had big bills for this date. There was a tussle with money exchange at the dollar van door. A twenty-dollar bill, she only had a twenty! Reserving the big bills for the date, properly distracted by prospects of Peggy's touch, she didn't think she had to pay since her last stop wasn't Empire, but court. Still, the rastaman didn't seem to agree. The side-boy at the door held his hand out.

She stood in the side aisle close to the door, and gave the sideman her $20 bill. "It's all I got," she said, forgetting to incorporate her patois. Everyone waited. Jan felt their eyes and ears against the sideboy's next step. Jan watched his hands, if they would ball up, if they would point to the door, if they would crumple her money. His hands would reveal his next move. His right palm waved to the driver.

"Driva, me need change fa twen-ty," the sideboy said turning to the rastaman affront the van. Driver only slightly turned his head, his hands hovering against a mound of rugged single dollar bills. One, two, three, four, five, rotated the slips of green between his thick fingers.

Jan glanced up toward the driver, not catching his face. At the red light, he seemed calm. "Sure ting boss," the Driver said to the side boy. A ten, a five, and three singles, were tapped into the side-boy's hands, then the door slid open. Others began to load out, waiting for another van, or finding the bus or the train. She turned to slap the back of the van, sealing it as complete to drive off. The spot where she lifted her hand, revealed the print of a paw from the lion of Judah, smudged against the tinted windows.

PRAIRIE BLUES

labl sarDyke

you forage for breath,
flick away my help, push
your pale self from the chair. i pat
and stretch the square of azure
fallen from your lap: wonky,
it won't lay flat. something erases
sixty years of skill, leaves hook, wool,
an unsalvable itch for competence in your hands.
dismissing water, food, questions,
you demand i *give back* your work.

memory slams its doors on nouns, names:
gust and edge collapse inside your words.
as an empty slope replaces the weight of the world
on your shoulders, the line is crossed:
your lips, dry and white, turn blue.

dense, navy veins pop between the freckles
of your hands as they flail
above your chest: here, pain. shrouded
in a secret language, wrapped inside
white sheets, attendants run you down the hall.

no blood clots reach the hearts' caverns
nor splatter your brain. they sit
in your lungs, red, slippery stories
withholding some end.

a week later sky still commands
inhalations so deep one barely

notices that glorious canopy change --
cobalt, delft, lapis -- those moments
of indigo that surrender to sliver and circle.
my body seeks night,
the stillness of moon, stars. breath,
returning from another galaxy,
reminds me sky created the palette for blue.

i shuffle into your room.
wrapped in your last afghan,
i watch you breathe. in a few hours
a new square, a different sky.

THIS THING NOT DEATH

lahl sarDyke

you regaled us with hot summer stories:
cousins swimming, jars of cray fish,
dismantling beaver damns, your hope
of accidental baptism into throngs
of family. you pressed against warm
limestone rocks, foot dangling in the river.

as children, you banned your daughters
to the shore; never hid your smile
when your sons returned from the other side.

on the last edges of winter, we sorted laundry,
polished floors, unpicked rows and rows of stitches,
threw the family's boots down the basement stairs.
heads bowed, we yearned for the bang and echo, the widening
cracks, the slow momentum of unwieldiness
as the river heaved, split, rushed into spring.

all those years when who kissed whose lips,
who held whose hand, mattered. you passed
the lace and veil over my head
to the youngest. i turned lovers inside out
not looking for you: petitions, placards,
armies of un-mothered daughters who did not fail.
i walked, cycled along that childhood river,
held my breath if i stopped at your door.

willing one foot in front of the other
i entered your room. death did not sit
in the chair by your bed. there was no sound

from the chemo drip. covering you in an afghan,
i slipped the book from your grey hands,
read aloud till we both imagined love.

i dreamt a river, long, smooth
with a crossing whose centre would hold us both.
on your side, rippled sands, a landscape breathing,
wide and waiting. on my side, gnarly oaks, blackberries,
an opulence of greens. we will meet arm-in-arm
rest with talk, a jar of ginger tea between us.
apples fill your pockets: skins so brilliant
i tremble. everywhere, a blue sky disperses light
with the generosity of pleased gods. striding
along opposite sides, laughter bounces
across the water. rounding the bend,
i watch the bridge disappear.

from the corner of my eye, your clothes,
hands, your hazel eyes begin their journey
toward sand and sky and light. cell by cell,
breath by breath, i'm left alone in my own skin.
when the earth rights, we are on her together,
but river is gone. you are leaving. i am grieving
and quietly, quietly dancing.

EMPTY

Caitlin Crowley

SISTER

Caitlin Crowley

AN ORDINARY WINDOW

Lynn Martin

It was extraordinary how that woman affected her. She would walk through a door, apology bending her body forward as if she had risked high winds or floods on her way, and was so, so sorry to be late. Emma remembered her arriving one day with a piece of twig tangled in her hair, conjuring up hollows, the tearing away of her very soul from wherever it was she had been. Then she would smile shyly and begin to talk. Everything would fade in the excitement of her stories. Emma would feel the tug of wayward currents, forceful undertows. A sudden explosion in the darkness would seduce her ear and Emma would surrender the entire world she knew just to follow Diana. Diana knew things. Oh yes, she knew things. Of course, all teachers knew things. And Emma was hungry to know things. Was that why writers of books always had been almost another species to her? Surely no one she knew wrote. Which might explain the mystery of the window. Not that the window was a mystery. It was an ordinary window in her house, a house she had inherited from her parents who had inherited it from their parents. The window overlooked the field in back of the house. Emma remembered the house as she had known it in her childhood; green and damp with a woodsy smell after a rain; the morning sunlight gilding every window to a glazed clarity. Now, of course, it was hers. It smelled of floors seldom washed. Cobwebs shimmered in corners. Since the death of her mother, five years ago, Emma had almost become a hermit. The house was large enough for her to wander from room to room at odd hours of the day. She would lean in a doorway, her hands folded across her breasts, and listen. But for what she didn't know. The back field sloped gently downward. There were two clumps of birch trees, one midway down, and the other almost at the bottom where a small stream separated her property from her neighbors. It was by the stream she saw Diana one morning just as the first light had crept half-way down the trees, but hadn't yet reached the surface of the water. She recognized Diana instantly, though at first she was nothing more than a shadow. How she was so sure the shadow was Diana she didn't know. Emma had stayed rooted by the window, convinced if she moved Diana would vanish. Ridiculous. There was no way Diana could see her. She was too far away. Besides no one could see in a window during the day. This was one of the qualities of windows Emma admired. And she knew she didn't want Diana to know how and where she lived. There was something about watching someone through a window, who couldn't see you, Emma had always secretly enjoyed. But it felt different this morning. As if Diana were aware of her standing there watching. Just then Diana turned and looked up the hill directly at the house as if in confirmation of Emma's thoughts. Emma panicked and hurried out of the room, away from the exposure, away from the window.

For she had things to do, she told herself. Her class met at four o'clock in the afternoon. She really thought it foolish to go back to school at fifty years old. Probably she never would have if it hadn't been for Candy's urging. Candy of the awful name, Emma thought. She cleaned for Emma once a week, just as she had previously cleaned for Emma's mother. Candy was nothing like her name. She was rail thin, tall and so full of nervous energy she could barely sit still for a shared teatime, a habit they had acquired through the years. Candy looked about as sweet as the Fire-thorn Bush out front, with its sharp thorns protecting its flaming berries. Candy's passion was talking, Continuously. Emma knew she talked even when there was no one else in the room. A table, a chair, a picture on the wall would do as well as a person.. At the time, Candy had stalked through the house lecturing the lamps, the drapes, the clock on the wall about people with secrets and strange ways. She swore Emma's mother would "turn over in her grave" over Emma's neglect of the house. Emma had ignored her, but Candy could wear you down much like a river eating away at a canyon over millions of years.

"You ought to do something with your life 'stead of moping around here. Must be something you want to do, other than wander around this house like a lost soul?" Both the question and Candy's voice hung in the air, waiting. She never gave up. "Ain't there?"

"Well, no," replied Emma, "not really."

Candy would then slam her teacup down with a crash and rush back to work, her shoulders slumped in disbelief and criticism. She would berate whatever caught her attention on Emma's foolishness and inability to see straight. The first time it had happened, Emma had replaced her mother's good china teacup with a dime store mug. Ten years later, she bowed to the flood and registered at the local community college. "Just to shut Candy up," she told herself.

It was all very bewildering. The only thing that made sense was the title of a book she'd seen on a teacher's desk. She wasn't even sure you called them teachers anymore. **All the women are white, all the men are black, but some of us are brave.** That was what was written on the cover of the book. "But some of us are brave," what a strange way to think of oneself, she thought. She supposed if she applied it to herself, she would have to say she wasn't. Everyone else seemed to rocket around what had once been an old grammar school with purpose and direction. Emma flattened herself against a wall and watched with scared eyes. When Diana had walked past and through a door, Emma had simply followed. Diana picked up a piece of chalk and began to write on the board when she turned and looked inquiringly at Emma. Emma had been astonished to hear a stranger using her voice say, " I'm new. I don't know where to go. Can I stay here?" Diana had merely pointed to a desk and returned her attention to the board. The sight of this dark haired, slightly dowdy woman, planted so firmly to the floor, soothed Emma. She signed up for the course that very night.

Well, it had worked. Candy was so full of questions about "schoolin", she no longer mentioned the house. Emma once again was free to stand in doorways and brood. Candy had never even come near to the whys of Emma's refusal to take proper care of where she lived. It wasn't, Emma knew, because she was rebelling against her mother, punishing her after death or any of that nonsense.

She'd once read a book about a daughter who couldn't do a thing because of her always interfering, dominating, terrible mother. "No," Emma thought, her mother hadn't been anything like that. An ordinary mother actually. Pleasant. Yes, she had been pleasant to live with. But somehow, her mother was so efficient in life, Emma had always felt inferior. She had tried to do the right thing. She had married, but it didn't hold. She hadn't even considered college. Women she knew didn't go to college.

Emma loved Diana's lectures on the short story. Diana talked about imagination as if it were an actual place she visited. All you needed, it seemed, was the right token and the subway doors would whoosh open at the proper stop; a pen would take you by the hand and you only had to follow. Emma struggled to understand this narrative of the unseen. Mostly she couldn't, but went with the rhythm of Diana's voice. She hated the bell that ended the class. It jangled Diana back to an ordinary woman. Emma would feel a giant fist toss her back into the classroom by the hairs on her neck, like the time they had given her gas to pull a tooth. She had dreamed of running and running, until something seized her and flipped her out of the darkness with a jolt that hurt unbearably. She would blink in the classroom's overhead lights, and watch while Diana gathered up her papers and almost ran out the door as if she ,too, were stunned, couldn't bear the eyes of the students, and needed to get away.

One night, with only two more classes to go, Diana had asked them to try and write a story themselves. Emma almost choked in trying to stifle her instant protest. She hadn't any story. Damn Candy. She should never have listened to her. Now what was she going to do?

In the next week, Emma went through reams of paper. She was drowning in round, crumpled balls rising at her feet like the underbellies of dead fish. Out of it, she had managed to write two pages. She had written about a cat who had wandered into her yard one day. How she had visited every house within miles trying to find it's owner. She struggled nightly with the task of putting words on paper. In class, she silently handed it in and fled. She didn't go to the next class.

But Emma met Diana again a week later. She was standing by the middle clump of birches on a night when the stars were dim and almost wiped out by a new moon. Diana leaned against the curved smoothness of bark, her hands quiet and her eyes darker than her hair, staring up at the house. Emma was stunned to see her. So much so, she didn't think to ask Diana what she was doing in her field. Or to ask her why she was staring at the window of her house. Emma turned and looked, trying to see what Diana was looking at. The moon was caught in the window's glass, squeezed even smaller by its frame. She thought she could see someone looking out the window, someone who looked like herself. Something sharp caught in her throat. She wanted to cry out to whoever it was. But she couldn't seem to move. Diana continued to stare at the window. She leaned into the shadow of the tree as if waiting for the moon to find its way out. Then she turned and smiled at Emma. Emma's first impulse was to run, but found herself unafraid in that direct gaze. She felt the moon slip free and land on her shoulder. She felt her entire body relax, her eyes take on the softness of the night. Of course Diana understood. She had brought the moon to show Emma how to escape the window. All she had to do was step outside.

Emma let Candy loose in the house. She transformed it in days. Cleaned and scrubbed it from floor to ceiling. They both went to the hardware store to choose new paint. There was only a small argument over whether it would be pale white, Emma's choice, or tangerine, Candy's choice. They compromised on tangerine walls and pale white woodwork. Emma bought a new desk and a brass floor lamp. That night she sat, pen in hand, and began,

It was extraordinary how that woman affected her. She would walk through a door, apology bending her body forward as if she had risked high winds or floods on her way, and was so, so sorry to be late.

LOOM

Kinnery Chaparrel

Imagine Arachne, shivering in astonishment and fear,
standing with thick bony uncovered knees, visible tibia,
held together, it seemed, by the very silk she intimately
used to weave her unowned body.

The people of Lydia fell prostrate and wept as their goddess
wove the faces of Olympus and Tartarus both, imperfect
eyes too weak to take in the trim of her masterpiece. Athena
used to weave her own gold body

when suspended in the stagnance of her fellow gods' perfection.
Faced with such beautiful stale options, how could she have justified
her unmatched skill, her inerrant thread, on anything but how she
used to weave her own pure body?

In the hovering infinity of deific life she grew
near desperate in the rust of unrivalled artistry; she had watched
Arachne grow beyond mortal skill, so she gave her the thread she
used to weave her newborn body,

and hovered silently above her bed at night, and gifted her
with visions of tapestries that human minds could never conceive.
How could she have known she would steal the blessed images Athena
used to weave her unknown body?

How could she say it was her ghost that played through this
mortal's naked lips, her shadow that made delight bloom from
Arachne's smile, her form that danced with her beneath sheets?
She could not claim the disguised hands she used to weave
between that body.

When Arachne finally left her loving muse dripping from the splintered pike of her pride, Athena could have wept a new sea, but she bent her body into a spindle and remembered how she used to weave her own body.

She dropped to earth, to confront the monster she had birthed in all her mortal beauty, and she hid her divine tears, and showed Arachne a cold and stony face, and did not betray warmth, or how she once used to weave her lover's body.

Athena called upon the people to judge the merit of their weaving, and didn't know whose agile hands she would bless lovingly, knowing only she would never love to weave again the way she used to weave this woman's body.

But the eyes of Lydia's people were too raw, and they could not take in the images that bled from Athena's wheel, and they were blinded at the sight of their own future, and the gods, how they once used to weave their mortal bodies.

Arachne, overwhelmed with both the beauty of her goddess' face and that her perfect hands could create, left to find the perfect tree to wrap such perfect thread around her throat, stronger than the
                                                                         thread she used to weave her sorry body.

Athena remained engrossed in her own art, unable to see Arachne's head hanging like a virgin dew drop from a linden tree, until her eyes bulged black and she cleaved the dangling
                                                                         limbs that she once used to weave her old body.

Athena raised her eyes once she'd finished her perfect tapestry
and saw her people on their knees, and Arachne hanging sorry
from her tree, and touched the girl, who shrank into the perfect
form now
used to weave her spider body.

It wasn't jealousy that brought Athena down from Olympus
to challenge her creation, nor sanctimony, but the hollow
strongroom in her chest — where she retired the loom which long
ago she
used to weave Arachne's body.

THE WIFE OF LOT

Kinnery Chaparrel

Who could blame her for turning back? The scent of warm unleavened bread could still be hanging among the blind bodies burning under the paved wreck, her hands might still be rough with the work of many weeks

and the sting of her married sons' melting flesh could have followed her to the cave where her grandsons were born. Women can't escape these things. She could have wrapped herself in the steady warmth of the only

two daughters she could save, but some holes never grow over, and the sutures had healed her husband's eyes closed, and what God would grant her flesh while burning her seed? Long before Lot, and angels' fingers on

her wrists, and ash in the air, she could remember her dreams. One night she had dreamt of holding a sack full of yeast, and pulling it to her chest, crushing it to her skin trying to fold it into her womb trying to solidify her

body against the wind, but the sack split and the yeast spilled and before she could gather it into her skirt the wind stole it and the yeast turned to flames as it hit the clouds. Perhaps as she turned, she was thinking of

this dream. Who could have resisted? Whether the fitful glow caught her eye, or she hoped you would salt the meat of your offerings with her flesh, this was martyrdom. This was penance. When you can't carry the mortar and limestone of your home on your back any longer, when the screams are impatient and bitter, sometimes it's worth one last look. I would have turned back too.

AM I?

E.M. Sheehan

1994

The girl's face looms above me, leering over the back of the school bus seat. She's probably an eighth-grader, given her air of confidence and the excessive amount of glittery eyeshadow.

"Are you a lesbian?" she asks me.

Um...what's a lesbian? Someone from the Middle East? I'm Italian and Okinawan and a host of other ethnicities, but Lesbian isn't one of them.

I've hesitated too long, and the girl is growing impatient. "Well? Are you?" Her tone is taunting, and her lips twist in a smirk. Maybe it's not an ethnicity after all. I feel like an idiot. This is probably something I should know. It's my first day of sixth grade, and I'm already behind the curve. I guess I might be a lesbian, since I'm not sure what that means, but I won't ask her for a definition and admit my ignorance. Based on her attitude, I suspect that there is a good answer and a bad answer to this question. What's the safest response?

Under her scrutiny, I squirm in my seat and blurt the truth: "I don't know."

The amusement in her eyes shows that I've made a serious blunder. "How can you not know? Either you are, or you aren't." She elbows the friend sitting next to her. "Guess what? This kid doesn't know if she's a lesbian." Giggles ensue, and the other girl's head pops up to stare.

My face feels hot enough to melt the green rubber seat. I press my thumb against the ridged impression someone else made with the heated top of a cigarette lighter, and pray that if I ignore these awful girls, they'll leave me alone.

"I bet she is," her friend says.

"Oh my God, you're a lesbian!" the first girl exclaims, loud enough that several heads across the aisle turn in my direction.

"No," I say quickly. Regardless of whether it's true, this is clearly what I should have said in the first place. "I'm not a lesbian."

"Are you sure?" she says. "I thought you didn't know."

"I'm sure," I say. Though of course, I have no idea.

1988

I'm playing *Candyland* with Mommy and Grandma. From the top of the stack, I pull the card with a picture of a snowflake and a beautiful lady dressed in blue. With a whoop of joy, I move my gingerbread-boy game piece all the way up to the snowflake square on the path.

I lean close to Grandma's ear and whisper, "I love Queen Frostine."

She smiles. "Me too! Look how close you are to winning. It's the luckiest card."

And the prettiest.

1990

The next two birthday presents in the pile are the unmistakable rectangular boxes which could contain nothing other than Barbie dolls.

Act happy, I remind myself. *Smile and say "thank you," like you mean it.*

But inside, I'm rolling my eyes. Anyone who knows me well knows that I'm not a Barbie doll kind of girl. They're too hard to dress and undress (especially the pants...what a pain!), and I've never understood why everyone else thinks they're fun. I humor my friends while we play with the Barbie collections at their houses, but I'm not jumping for joy at the thought of having my own.

I tear the wrapping off the first box, and as it turns out, I don't have to force a smile. It's not just any old Barbie doll...it's Ariel. Ruby-red hair, shimmery green tail.

"I heard you like The Little Mermaid," my aunt says.

"I do! It's my favorite movie. Thank you."

Predictably, the second box contains Eric. Big whoop. It's Ariel I care about. In my opinion, she's the best Disney princess. She's not helpless. She doesn't just let stuff happen to her. She knows what she wants, and she risks everything to get it. And in the beginning, *she* saves the prince! Gutsy, beautiful, and a great singing voice. She's awesome.

I play with that Ariel doll a lot in the months after my birthday. Unlike Barbie's pants, her fins slip on and off easily, transforming her from the mermaid she's supposed to be into the woman she wants to become. I brush her silky, fiery tresses. Gosh, I love that red hair.

I wish Ariel was real, so I could meet her. I think it would be really nice if she were part of my world.

1996

Ridiculous stuff happens in dreams. I've dreamt that I turned into a mermaid, but that doesn't mean I want to be one (although that would be pretty cool). Anyway, it doesn't matter that I dream about kissing girls and not boys, because I have a boyfriend and I kiss him in real life. Sometimes we do more than kiss. I'm willing to try almost anything, but I won't sleep with him. I'm only thirteen, and good little Catholic girls wait until marriage. Or at least until college.

He never pushes me farther than I'm willing to go, but lately there are times when I want him to leave me alone altogether, and I can hardly stand to be touched. I end our kisses sooner. He tries to give me a backrub, but I pull away and ask him to stop. I see the hurt in his eyes, but I have to put space between us when I feel this way. I can't help it.

I thought it would be like trying a new food. The first time, it's weird. The second time, it's tolerable. The third time, it's pretty good. The fourth time, it's delicious. Except that the longer I'm with him, the more it seems to be working in reverse. He's less appetizing with each taste. I can tell he wants me more than I want him. He craves me. I enjoy wielding that kind of power over him, but as the novelty fades, so does my interest.

When I'm with him, it's never as good as my dreams. But dreams aren't real, so this is as good as it gets.

1997

I've seen *Titanic* in the theater five times. My friends and I gush over Leonardo DiCaprio, like all the other high school girls on the planet. He's hot. Everyone thinks so.

"I like his eyes," I say, remembering the look in those baby blues as he studied Rose over the top of the paper, drawing her in the nude. But now I'm picturing Kate Winslet's bare breasts, and I feel my cheeks flush. "Leo's eyes are sexy."

I am *not* a lesbian.

Ellen DeGeneres is a lesbian. Melissa Etheridge is a lesbian. That's all well and good for them, but not me.

2000

I rush to the locker room with a crowd of dripping, swimsuit-clad girls, vying for a shower nozzle with good water pressure. We have five minutes before the first bell and ten minutes before we have to be in our next classes. That's not a lot of time to shampoo and condition, strip and dress, and fix hair and makeup, all while trying to maintain modesty. I'm doing my best to hurry when a flash of red catches my eye. My hands slow their scrubbing. I can't look away.

I've noticed her before, of course. She has the most perfect body I've ever seen on a real girl who isn't a model or a movie star. It would be impossible not to notice and admire, as one might admire other works of nature—a rosy sunrise, a crystal-clear lake, an exquisite blossom. Surely I'm not the only girl in this room who can appreciate her flawless hourglass figure, her perky boobs, her stretchmark-free, tanned skin.

Normally, I don't let myself look too long, forcing my eyes to skim past her. Not because she might catch me staring. I know she won't. She's a cheerleader, one of the popular girls, so by design her vision is tunneled. She doesn't see the shy, nerdy girl on the periphery. She probably doesn't even know my name. I'm not afraid of being caught, I just don't want to be a creep. And after the initial admiration other feelings will follow that are best ignored. Feelings that make me a creep, if I let them happen.

But today, I can't stop watching her. She's gotten a haircut since the last gym class. Her former shoulder-length, strawberry-blonde locks are cropped into a sleek, shapely bob. The style complements her delicate cheekbones and jawline, and accentuates her long, slender neck. And she's dyed it a stunning shade of reddish-gold. It's the color that pins my attention. I'm a sucker for redheads.

She raises her hands and massages a dollop of shampoo into that gorgeous hair. When her arms come up, her taut nipples strain against the spandex of her suit. She closes her eyes and rinses, and the suds course down her neck and chest, disappearing between her breasts.

A wave of tingling heat spreads throughout my body, my stomach quivers, and I feel a wetness that has nothing to do with the shower. I've looked too long. Trembling, I close my eyes and take a step backward under the cascading water to wash away my shame.

"The bell's going to ring," my friend calls. "Are you coming?"

Nearly. I release a small, shaky breath. "Yes. I'm almost done."

2001

Maybe I'm bisexual. I'd be okay with that. It's better to be bi than a lesbian, because if I choose to be with a man, no one will ever find out how I feel about women. If I don't act on it or tell anyone about it, then I'm really no different than my heterosexual siblings and friends. And now that I'm in college, there's tons of guys to choose from. Way more than in high school. Surely I'll be able to find a man who makes my heart race, who makes me happy enough that I'll forget I ever wanted anyone else.

2002

After a year and a half of awkward flirting and forgettable first dates, I finally have a boyfriend again. A sweet, sensitive guy. He's fun, attentive, polite, and geeky in an adorable way. Unintimidating. Comfortable. There's only one problem: when we're intimate, I'm not aroused. I don't feel any passion at all. It feels like a chore, and although it's not much different than any other time I've been with a guy, I thought I'd be better at it by now. I bring up the subject of sex, but in a half-hearted sort of way. We haven't been together very long, and neither of us are ready. I'm relieved when we agree to wait. I'd only suggested it because I'd hoped it might help me feel closer to him. I don't know what I need to make me feel the way I should. Nothing's wrong, but nothing seems quite right either.

During a hot and heavy make-out session a few months into our relationship, my mind wanders. I'm bored, and that worries me. When I try to refocus, a little voice in the back of my head whispers, *Let me help you. Picture this: Her gentle, stubble-free kisses caress your lips. You breathe the sweet, intoxicating scent of her perfume as you run your tongue down her neck, her collarbone, her breasts. You pause to circle a nipple and take it into your mouth, eliciting a gasp and a high-pitched moan. She arches her back, begging to be touched. Your palm cups the fleshy curve of her hip. Your fingertips skim across her smooth-shaven thigh, sliding to the center of her soft, wet desire. There you go...that's better, isn't it? This is what you want. What you need.*

The fantasy makes me ache. I'm so turned on right now. His body may be angular and hairy and hard, his moans deep and rumbling, but if I close my eyes and transform him with my mind, I can hold onto this feeling...

Like a rubber band stretched to the breaking point, an internal stinging slap jolts me back to reality. This is ludicrous. I'm with an attractive, perfectly decent guy, but I can't enjoy it unless I imagine he's a woman? What the hell is wrong with me? The answer punches me in the gut and steals my breath: I'm not bisexual. I'm not attracted to men at all. I never have been, and never will be.

I'll never be like everyone else. I won't have a normal wedding or a normal family. People will treat me like that girl on the school bus: *Look at the weirdo. Let's point and laugh.* It's the last thing I want, but as it turns out, I don't have a choice. I've tried to ignore it and pretend to be someone I'm not, and it doesn't work. I'm miserable, and I can't keep lying to my boyfriend or to myself. It's not fair to either of us. Distraught and crying, I dump him without warning or explanation aside from the awful "It's not you, it's me" excuse. This isn't my finest hour, but I'm not in my right mind. I can't begin to describe shattered mess inside my head. He deserves to be treated better than this. I hope that someday, he'll understand.

I'm just a lost, frightened girl who is everything she never wanted to be, who can't bring herself to use the words that would provide definition and clarity because they'll make her the brunt of the joke. I'm that little sixth-grader, burning with shame and wishing I could disappear.

2003

Thank God for free, university-sponsored therapy. After several counseling sessions, I'm taking baby steps toward accepting who I am, and making peace with it. I'm no longer living a lie, but even after I've come out to myself, I don't come out to many people. Some of my hesitation is driven by fear of their reactions, but the truth is, I don't like using the L-word. Naming it aloud and claiming it as my own makes me feel sick to my stomach. But I tell a handful of trusted friends, and it gets a little easier each time. Still, the word sticks in my throat.

I haven't told my family yet. Half of them are ultra-conservative and religious. They will not approve, so I'll come clean on a strictly need-to-know basis. Until I'm in a serious relationship with a woman, they don't need to know. When they ask probing questions about boyfriend prospects, I say I'm not seeing anyone at the moment, and leave it at that. I'll tell them when I have to, and not a minute sooner.

2005

I'm in love. When she's near, my heart races. When we're apart, I can think of nothing but her. I crave her kisses. She makes me feel whole.

We want to live together after I graduate. In a few months, we will move to my hometown, which means that I have no choice but to come out to my family. It won't be easy, but I want a future with her, so it will be worth it. We will create our own version of normal.

2016

I've won many battles in my fight for love and self-acceptance. I have a wife, my son has two moms, and I proudly share this information with the world. My sexual orientation is no longer a secret, and I am no longer ashamed to live the life I was born to lead, and to love the way I was meant to love.

And yet, twenty-two years after that school bus ride, I still have trouble saying those four little words aloud: *I am a lesbian.*

THIRST

Madari Pendás

David bent over the bed and grabbed his other navy blue dress sock. As he put his foot into the sock his toe slipped out. All his socks had holes in them. He folded over the top of the material and put his foot into his loafer.

"Can I have a water from the mini bar?" Julie asked as she swirled her ponytail into a bun.

"Those are too expensive, I have water in the car, get dressed," David said.

Julie, who had already opened the mini bar, put the bottle of water back. She picked up her underwear and wiggled it up her thighs. David smiled at her, his salesman smile, where only his lips stretch and the rest of his face remains unchanged. It's the smile David gave Amy the day he proposed; the smile he gave when he was the only one at his manager's funeral who wasn't crying; the smile he flaunts the homeless when he says he has no change, yet his pockets jingle.

Julie was young and pretty, when he walked with Julie other men turned their heads—David loved that. He'd lay his hand on Julie's ass as they walked, and watched the men's faces turn to disappointment or, even better, envy. With Amy no one looked.

Julie watched as cars pulled in, she saw some families with luggage and looks of hopeful expectation, and others couples walking a distance apart.

"How's Amy? She showed me a painting she did last week. It was of a lake. It was beautiful," Julie asked, never taking her eyes off the window.

"Fine, I guess," David said. He walked to the stand next to the bed and pulled a drawer. On top of a Gideon Bible was his wedding band, which he struggled to get on his finger.

David walked into the bathroom and examined his neck. He walked back out of the room and reached into Julie's purse and grabbed brown foundation.

"Help me out, will ya?"

Julie sauntered into the bathroom, still thinking of Amy. She used her thumb to blend the foundation with David's skin tone. David extended his neck so Julie could conceal the other love marks. She passed her thumb over his Adam's apple and pressed into it. He recoiled; she shrugged apologetically and returned to hiding the infidelity from his body.

"Room service," a voice said.

David walked over and unlocked the door.

"Wait! We didn't order room service," Julie said.

Amy rushed into the room, pushing David between the door and the wall.

"I can explain," David said rushing to Amy and grabbing her hand.

"How could you?" Amy asked.

"Baby, I'm sorry, let's talk about this at home."

Amy pushed his hands away and walked past David towards Julie.

"How could you do this to me?"

"It was a mistake. It didn't mean anything," Julie said.

"Why him?" Amy asked

"I don't know."

"You ruined us!"

"I didn't expect any of this, let's go and talk. We can fix this."

Amy scowled and tried to exit. Julie blocked the exit and wrapped her arms around Amy, who resisted her body.

"You can't un-break this, or un-fuck it up."

"I'm sorry. I love you, please don't go," Julie pleaded, kissing Amy's neck and chin.

"You said you didn't even like men!"

David watched from the entrance of the bathroom and walked towards Amy.

"You're cheating on me?" David asked.

"Yes, David, I am. I'm just like you. We even have the same taste in women."

David grabbed his briefcase and walked out; but returned to slam the door harder to, accent his exit. Amy dropped to her knees. Julie kissed Amy's palm and gripped them tightly. Julie whispered faint apologizes, like a devoted monk in her repetitions, speaking the only words her mind could fathom and produce. Amy weaseled out of Julie's embrace and walked towards the mini bar. She examined Julie's trembling and anxious body and grabbed a bottle from the refrigerator. She took a swig, let out a long exasperated breath and turned to Julie.

"Do you want some water?"

CHANCES ARE

Kai Coggin

I went to my first gay bar
when I was 18
snuck into this 21 and up
saloon hip hop combo club
called Chances
in the gay heyday of Montrose
before gentrification
wrapped its white claws
around everything rainbow

Chances was a lesbian bar
filled to the rafters with young baby dykes
and older butches who had their lives together
gripping tight to their pseudo-wives
or lonely hearts holding hands with bud light bottles
sizing up the femmes fluttering around
like butterflies in the dark rooms
possible two step partners
late night hook ups
tender kisses in corners
hands
bodies
cheeks
hips finding a place to be safe
to move
free

at 18
I looked
like a boy

wore men's clothes
baggy pants
button up shirts
got called sir at the grocery store
filled in for my absent father as the man of the family
my hair so short that I had a fade around the sides
hiding everything female about myself
after it was taken away by the hands of a stranger at 13

I snuck into Chances
with my cool older friend Heather
using her friend's expired drivers license
so excited and scared but trying to act calm
nonchalant
no, I am not sneaking in
yes, I come here all the time

Joe Allen Henry was his full name
but just call me Joe
had to memorize his address
and birthday in case the cops got wise to me
my baby face brown eyes wide with
this new world of women like me
loving women like me
holding each other
laughing together
dancing in a circle
around the tight dance floor
lights flashing
a disco ball
this was the nineties after all
and the closet was home to so many
not like now

but back then
chances are this was sanctuary
chances are this was escape
chances are this was the only place where it was okay
for a woman to love another woman in public

the night is fuzzy now as I look back twenty years
think I might've had a beer or two
might've two-stepped to a George Straight song with a stranger
might've smiled too wide that my adolescence showed
before the bulky butch female cop
moseyed over to me and asked for my ID
she eyed the card
eyed me

Joe Allen Henry, huh?
her badge flashed in the strobes
to the rhythm of the pumping music
she looked me up and down
my hands stuffed my pockets
head down
neck turtling into my starched collar
I was discovered
the jig was up
the man
     was just a girl
trying to find a place
to dance

the butch cop was kind to me
just shook her head and said   *you are using a man's ID?*
shame shot through me but turned to
knowing she was trying to tell me I didn't have to pretend

that the time would come
and I would be my real self someday
chances are she had been in my shoes a couple of decades back
chances are she knew how it felt to want to belong
chances are we had more in common
than holding the world heavy on our shoulders

I left without a fight
with a smile on my face
and just three years to wait
before I could come back to be safe in this space

chances are
I danced around that two-step dance floor
hundreds of times over the years
grinded my hips to other soft hips on the hip-hop side
shot pool there on Tuesday afternoons after work
always a bottleneck in my hand
cigarette smoke in my eyes
stood on the sidelines
as a woman I loved
danced with all the other girls but me
shaped my heartache into tangible numbing
learned my own ability to make a joke
to replace the rejection
chances are this place became a theater for my splayed-out sadness
chances are I cried into my beer more than once

there was a huge fire at Chances in 2006
the owner wanted to spend more time fishing with his son
didn't want to rebuild I heard
and everything in Montrose changed over time
there is an upscale wine bar called *underbelly*

that stands on its foundation today
gentrified all the gay away

this is a time in my life that seems so far
from who I am now
almost another lifetime
I had to be so tough
had to cling so hard to an identity
because I spent so much time in my youth hiding it
I loved someone for eight years
who never loved me enough to hold my hand
or dance with me or call me hers... at Chances

chances are it made me feel unworthy of love
chances are I thought this is what I deserved
until I met real love face to face
and the whole world became my dance floor

I cracked out of that tough boy's body
and became a woman
underneath the stars of someone who saw my light
but all these pains
were just part of the fight
the dance around the floor of my own karma
the settling of debts
from hearts I must've broken in other lives
and every heartache I remember in this life
I use as a tool to help others some how

how else can we grow
from the memories that shape us?

chances are I just needed to be loved

and now I am

but more importantly   I love myself

chances are
somewhere out there tonight
there is a young girl
with a man's ID
sneaking into her first gay club
too scared to ask another girl to dance

chances are
if I saw her I would reach out my hand
pull her close
and whisper in her ear
wait
wait
it gets better, dear

WHO WILL KNOW

Michelle E. Brown

Who will know
Know that while I still walk
My pace has slowed a bit
I stop to smell the roses
Watch the seasons change
That I arrive a little late
No longer painfully punctual
Just a little late
With stories to tell
Of things I saw
Along the way.

Who will know
The stories I tell again
And again
Listening patiently
Giving me a loving nudge
When I get stuck along the way
The words hanging on the tip of my tongue
Reminding me of my memories
When my words begin to fail

Who will know
That I need a helping hand
When my cozy clutter has become just a mess
Maybe looking a little disheveled
Or even unkempt
When my pride keeps me from saying
I can't
So I hide,

Simply staying inside
Living alone, being alone
Because I'm alone

Who will know
When time is running short
Help me savor every moment
Take one more walk in the sun and rain
Listen to my stories
Helping fill in all the wholes
Share another laugh,
Another dance
Another hug
Another tear

Who will know
When I'm ready to cross over
To face that grand adventure
Remind me my work is over
Remind me that I have loved
And am loved
Then as we listen to music
Just sit and hold my hand

Who will know
When I start to believe
I know

Will you?

LOVE OF MY YOUTH 1

Sierra Schweitzer

LOVE OF MY YOUTH 2

Sierra Schweitzer

Artist Statement: These photographs capture the blossoming love between my girlfriend and I in the early stages of our relationship. While trying on my great grandmother Violetta's beautiful handmade Italian dresses, and then later on a gazebo in Southport, NC, I truly caught the 'Love of my Youth' in her entirety.

THE GOLD ROOM

Lee Lynch

There were murmurs, there was laughter, the piano man performed with his usual light, sophisticated touch. Leather banquettes lined the walls and the beveled room dividers were polished to an apricot hue. With minimal pretention, The Rinaldi family's Gold Room was glamorous, a *ristorante di lusso*—a fancy restaurant.

At thirty-six, Fritzie Rinaldi was raring to take over. She'd been on the loud, brash side as a child, narrow-shouldered, ham-handed, as if her body couldn't decide what form it should take. The kids she fought called her "Fritzie" for good reason, after Fritzie Zivic, a white boxing champ known for dirty fighting.

Her parents put her to work at the restaurant as a deterrent to bad behavior, and she took to the work—the natural heir to the business rather than her brothers Dom and Sal, who wanted only to be ironworkers. Bit by bit, she grew taller, her voice softened, and, in the dining area, her manner eased.

Fritzie lifted the reserved sign from a corner table. On the starched and monogrammed linen cloth, a small gold-tasseled lamp glowed. High overhead hung brass and crystal chandeliers. The pianist nodded to them as he played Fritzie's personal theme song, "The Impossible Dream."

"This is always such a treat, Fritzie," whispered Edie. "My mouth is watering."

Esther patted Fritzie's shoulder and said, "Thank you."

Fritzie Rinaldi seated Colette, her lover of twelve years, and their two best friends. Edie Velardi had grown up three houses from Fritzie, in Queens, and never moved out of her late parents' row house. Instead, Esther Barber moved in, the first African American in the neighborhood. The street had changed over time, but not by much, not in its heart, like the Gold Room, which remained the classic it had been in 1939 when Fritzie's grandfather passed it down to Fritzie's father who now entrusted it to her.

They caught up with their comings and goings as the busser poured ice water into signature glassware trimmed with gold.

Esther and Colette sat with their backs to the room because Fritzie was always on the job. She watched the servers' every move, the presentation of the food, the reliably favorable reactions of the well-dressed diners.

Behind the scenes, she became as impatient and hard to please as her father. The well-paid kitchen and wait staff were renowned for consistent quality and speed; she pledged never to allow a decline in The Gold Room's flawless reputation. Her grandparents designed the sixty-seat dining room as an elegant sanctuary from the bedlam of the city, with thick gold carpeting and tufted leather wall panels. Fritzie's grandparents liked to say, when you entered the Gold Room, you left the city.

Fritzie said, "I wanted to tell Colette and you girls about a little problem I ran into downtown."

Esther played the joker among them. "Is one of your fans following you again?"

"We're all-too used to that," said Colette, surreptitiously removing gum from her mouth and into her purse with a tissue.

Colette Galveston was the great, great granddaughter of a slave taken to Texas from Virginia. Later, he was set free in the rollicking Wild West city from which he took his name. The men in the family worked on the wharves, or rode off to herd cows, and intermarried with the hodgepodge of newcomers. Colette barely had enough fingers to count the racial strains in her blood. Short and full-bodied, thick dark hair curling this way and that, her skin was lighter than her Italian-American lover's. Her accent was deeply East Texas.

Colette had come north with her gospel choir for a competition, explored the bars with a gay buddy, and never lived in Texas again.

She worked in music ministries around the city by day. Nights, until recently, she'd been stage manager a the club where Fritzie performed.

Edie and Esther pronounced them a good match the first time they all got together. As Edie said, at times Colette seemed to cushion the world from Fritzie; at other times, she cushioned Fritzie from the world.

Fritzie held up a finger and glided, in her black vest and slightly flared black slacks, to another table, where she talked and laughed with three businessmen who, monthly, ate at The Gold Room before their poker game. She called for a replacement when a napkin slipped off a woman's lap, then bowed to delighted thanks as she backed away with her performer's grace.

Esther shook her head. "The way she moves, Fritzie is an athlete."

"She must be the first female *maître d'* in the city," said Edie. It was only 1958.

Fritzie chatted with another table of diners. Colette said, "She used to get so mad at her parents when they introduced her as their hostess. There's something in Fritzie that can't bear feminine frills, though she doesn't hanker to be anything except a woman. Look at my woman: debonair come to life. Makes me want to take her home and..."

The waiter, who wore an impossibly white jacket and a black bow tie, served a basket of warm bread and a bowl of herbed olive oil dip. Fritzie rejoined them. As if she'd never interrupted herself, she said, "I got a call today. The new owners of the club aren't happy with my act."

"Bull puckey," said Colette. "You make them piles of money."

Fritzie moonlighted as resident drag king at the Tuckaway Club downtown. She leaned toward Edie and Esther. "They took complete control of the club's management, including Colette's position."

"Bad enough they laid *me* off," Colette said, "but you're a big draw. I'll go down there after dinner and light a fire under those queens. They need to go on strike."

Fritzie winced. "Hold your Texas horses, Colette. First off, some of the queens desperately need that income. Second, for every guy working there, a dozen more want to be. Third, no one's firing me." She paused, moved her silverware infinitesimally straighter, and looked up with a quick flimsy smile. "They want to spiff the act up, make me a female as well as a male impersonator."

The table went silent against the background of soft conversations, a man's wheezy cough. Someone smoked a cigar; Esther pinched her nose shut against the smell.

"I have the voice for it," Fritzie protested into the silence.

A strong contralto, fans said she outperformed the men. She specialized in crooners. As a kid, her father encouraged her to imitate singers for guests. She did them on stage now: Sinatra, Bing Crosby, Frankie Laine, Perry Como. She spoofed Dean Martin and danced while she sang Fred Astaire songs, taking the lead with any available queen. A couple of them towered over her—that number got laughs every time. She did a lot with a fedora, a light pole prop and a cane.

"Make believe you're a guy in a gown? That would turn the tables for sure," said Esther, no longer laughing.

Colette fiddled with the pearl cluster earrings Fritzie gave her for their tenth anniversary. She asked, "How do you plan to pull off that trick?"

"You don't know the first thing about dressing like a girl, girl," said Esther.

"Doesn't matter. I work with New York drag performers—the experts."

Edie's mouth shaped an "O." She said, "Imagine the gowns."

"I don't even want to," said Colette, with a sorrow her friends last saw when she returned from Texas after her mother's death.

While Edie might love beautiful gowns, she worked as a school counselor. This wasn't the first time her skills had come in handy over the years. "Fritzie, might this be a good point to take a break from performing and concentrate on your new role here at the restaurant?"

"*Fuori di testa*," said Fritzie. "You're crazy as a loon. The club *is* my break, Edie. I let off steam downtown. It makes me mad as hell, us living as if we're criminals hiding from the law. What's so wrong with me? I'm an honest, hard-working citizen, just like these squares. You think I *want* to pretend I'm a chanteuse? I have to, to stay on stage at the club. Don't make it harder for me."

The snooty wine steward, who Fritzie pined to replace, arrived. She made a brusque gesture for him to pour, skipping the proffered tasting ritual, an unheard-of omission for her. They'd already partaken of cocktails in the bar at the front of the restaurant, where Colette and Edie briefly became tipsy and silly, but you didn't say no to Fritzie's largesse.

"They won't force you to do that, right?" Colette said. "Do I make my choir kids preach sermons instead of singing hymns?"

Esther stopped pulling at her bottom lip. "You know, Fritzie, it might be a hoot for a person to do it once. Other than that, Colette's right, it's not you. I'd squirm simply watching."

"Exactly," said Colette. "It would be a sin against God and nature."

Fritzie slapped the table with the flat of her hand hard enough to slosh the wine in their glasses. "I may have more sides than you know."

Edie's eyes caught the light from the chandeliers. "I've always dreamed of owning an evening gown."

Esther seldom drank. When she got tight, she spoke in mumbles. "You have?"

"If you switch to gowns, lover girl," said Colette, "how do you spell d-i-v-o-r-c-e?"

"Who will I harm doing this? The squares?" Fritzie's aggravated voice squeaked.

"To hell with the squares. You'd damage my one and only you."

Edie knew the wisdom of retreat. "Come on, Colette. Let's go to the powder room."

After the two left, an old woman in diamonds and bulky hearing aids passed.

Fritzie raised her voice. "You look like a million dollars, Mrs. Pope."

"Quite a charmer, our young Miss Rinaldi," said the woman. "I've known this child," she told Esther, "since her papa counted her age in weeks."

Their waiter arrived with a round tray balanced over his shoulder.

"Hold the appetizers until the ladies return, please, Byron."

Byron bowed his head and backed away.

Fritzie said, "He's a dancer and he promised to help me learn to follow. If I can stomach it."

Esther raised an eyebrow.

"So, tell me, Esther, what's with my Colette? Am I dead? No. Have I left her? No. Do I need to change the act to keep my downtown life? Yes. So, I have to compromise here and there. Doesn't everyone?"

"Not you, of all people. Edie's told me stories of you filching clothes from her Cousin Nick."

Fritzie tapped her wine glass with a severely clipped fingernail.

"Let me ask you, Fritz. Who did Colette fall for years ago?"

"What do you mean, who? Me, of course."

"Which you? The drag king or a lady in a gown?"

"Hell, Colette has seen me in a skirt before. I'm still me."

"You know I'm not talking about clothes for a family do, Fritzie. What those owners want from you—can you live with that?"

"I don't know, Es, maybe the straights, seeing us, will get used to us, treat us better outside the clubs someday."

"What are you—some kind of savior?"

"Yeah, that's me alright. Seriously, though, the new owners? Her daddy gave them the business as a wedding gift. Now they have to make it pay and come up with this doozy. My ladies, the queens, are dying for me. They'd shred anyone who tried to hurt me. Not to mention, I can handle myself." She brandished her still out-sized fists. "This is a different sort of hurt. Drag is how I'm able to be the me in here." Fritzie struck her chest with a fist. "*Capice?* That stage is my real life sometimes. The owners want to cash in—"

"—on your queer soul. That's what they want to cash in on."

Fritzie bent her head to her hands, and massaged her forehead with her fingers. "You're right, Es. It's one thing to wear a tailored skirt and oxford shirt, but turning myself into a showgirl is like putting a subway car on an airport runway and clearing it for flight."

"I'm telling you, Fritz, it's a non-starter."

The waiter helped Colette and Edie into their seats again. Colette smoothed and smoothed the linen napkin on her lap as if that would prolong her calm.

Esther said, "What if Colette skipped the show?"

"That's a given." Fritzie covered Colette's hand with her own, just for a second. "I don't want any of you in the audience, especially my *gattina*, my kitten."

"I'd rather see you thrown off a bull in the rodeo than all dolled up."

Fritzie set both fists on the table. "If I refuse, there's plenty who'll line up to replace me, Colette."

"Meanwhile, you'll come home from shows sad as a hound dog's eyes and complain for a week before every performance."

"So, you want me to drop it? Lose my gig altogether?"

They glared at each other like enemies.

"Girls, girls," said Edie. "Accept them or not, Fritzie, you have our opinions. Let's let this go for the moment and enjoy ourselves."

Colette leaned back in her seat. "Good idea, Edie. We don't want to ruin your wild and crazy night on the town."

All four laughed. Fritzie winked at Colette, told the wine steward to bring a second bottle, and the waiter arrived with the appetizers. "You'll love this new *carpaccio*," she said, indicating the paper-thin slices of raw beef, capers, and onions, wet with olive oil and lemon juice.

Esther and Edie exchanged glances. In the way of these aged New York luxury restaurants, the Gold Room's menu never changed. Yet change it Fritzie had.

"Yeah," said Esther. "This is fine eating, very fine."

They joked around, cheerful and giddy after the testy words.

"Get a load of that dress," Esther mumbled to Fritzie as she indicated with her eyes an arriving diner. "Will you wear a number like that one?" Her laughter unruly with drink, she outlined a womanly shape with her hands.

"Stop it!" Colette stage whispered.

Edie lay a hand on Colette's shoulder. "It's the restaurant, Colette. Fritzie's taking over a third-generation family business and she's the first woman to do it. She has to balance acting straight with—"

"I know all that, Edie. Tell me, for Fritzie, where's the balance if she's no longer a king, but a queen?"

Esther said, "I was kidding you, Fritzie, about wearing that dress. You're no snake—you can't shed your skin."

"Ladies," said Fritzie. "Picture the whole sequence. First the drag king tour de force, then the female bit, and, presto, I'm a drag king again, then presto once more, I'm a woman from the get-go."

Colette shook her head. "A freak show. That's what the owners want, not respectful drag, not you being your real self on stage. *Au contraire*, they're after cheap laughs at our expense."

"Who else can I be other than my real self?"

"That's what I'm afraid to find out."

"How is it different from what we do every day—faking it?"

###

Five months later, the two couples sat in the same corner, heard the same songs, were served another superb dinner in the hushed splendor of The Gold Room. Typical of Fritzie, she'd assumed she was indomitable; she'd gone ahead with preparations for her new act.

After the entrée, Fritzie excused herself. Thinner, her smile dimmed, she walked a little slower. A small girl watched from the entryway. Fritzie held out her arms and waltzed the girl to her seat.

"The child expects this now," Colette explained. "And I swear it's one of the things that's bringing Fritz back to life, these rituals with her regulars."

"A complete breakdown?" asked Edie.

"Admission to the hospital and all."

Byron the waiter presented the watermelon pudding, a house specialty. Fritzie sat and picked at the chopped pistachios and curls of dark chocolate atop her dessert. Without any preface, in a bitter manic burst, Fritzie told them what happened.

"It's a sellout act; I'm breathing easier because I don't have to do it. The owners gave it to a straight unemployed actress at twice my pay. She can't sing for shit. She lip-syncs to recordings the new owners made—" She brought a fist to her mouth, kept it there, silent.

"They recorded Fritzie without telling her," said Colette, leaning forward over the table, brandishing a spoon. "The SOBs stole her voice."

Fritzie opened her eyes, slammed her fists onto her thighs. "From what I hear, the goddamned audience eats it up. She's drawing in more straights and tourists. Byron told me Colette, in heels and a chignon, could do a better drag king."

For once, Fritzie didn't watch the room. She sucked her lips inward over her teeth. Fritzie wasn't one to cry—certainly not at work.

Colette curled a quick hand over Fritzie's shoulder. With a deep breath, Fritzie raised her head. "The guys unveiled the sparkly gown they made for me. They called it a work of art—much showier than I expected: frilly, dainty, lacy, fussy. They understood I was thrown for a loop, but to them that's show biz. There were nylons, a garter belt and a built-up brassiere on a chair."

"Jesus, Mary and Joseph," said Esther, crossing herself.

"How can anyone stand that greasy lipstick? The foundation base stank and was suffocating. Sweat boiled out of the rest my body. I thought I ate bad food and went into the staff bathroom, got sick, held a wet paper towel to the back of my neck. In the mirror, I saw a creature in makeup hatched from the Gowanus Canal.

"I saw the wigs when I went back. The guys were more than good to me. They knew I was messed up and took it slow. Two more queens came in to prep for their acts. Of course, they wanted to help too. The examination and comments, kindly meant, got to me. The cosmetics ran. I had the shakes.

"I looked in the dressing room mirror and again didn't find myself. My vision went blurry, I plunged past the boys, crashed through the door to the alley. Earlier, a plow piled snow up against the buildings and I rubbed it over my wrists, my face, gulped cold air till my lungs burned.

"How many masks can a person wear? I should have listened to the three of you. I've had my fill of masquerades."

Edie said, "Yet you wear a tie in the Gold Room."

Fritzie touched her black bow tie, the same one the servers wore. "Because it's me, Edie. A tie builds me up, gives me super powers. This doesn't sound crazy to you, Esther, does it?"

Esther shook her head as Fritzie spoke. "I understand; I'm trying to put it in words. Like me, it's not that Fritzie wants to be a man; she needs to be her kind of woman. Cosmetics and gowns are Edie's kind of woman. Dyed leather skirts and low-cut tops are

Colette's. Every day, I can't wait to strip off my teacher drag and pull on jeans and a shirt. Fritzie's woman is tailored, with a classy guy style. Anything else gives her—what do you call it, Fritzie—*agita?*"

"Clothes represent self-identity." Edie sounded completely sober. "Your identity is very strong, Fritzie, even though—or because— it's been under constant derision and criticism your entire life."

"So, she's likely to get all shook up when it's threatened?" Esther asked.

"That makes sense," said Colette.

Fritzie's face had aged into sadness since their last visit.

Colette tugged Fritzie's silk pocket square from her vest and offered it to her, saying, "She walked the whole way home to me that night and, what you predicted, Esther, happened, she fell apart. For weeks, I went to work with her and made myself useful."

Fritzie patted her eyes with the pocket square. "Not once did Colette leave my side. My brain shorted out. Coming to The Gold Room became an ordeal I endured rather than lose my parents' trust. They don't have the faintest idea about the Tuckaway Club. Colette prompted me to watch this and do that. She kept the place running."

"Oh, come on, I may have nudged you here and there."

Fritzie stared at the table, rubbing a tear from her cheek. "That woman I tried to play, that fake—*I'm* the woman, not her." She met Esther's eyes. "The thought of the club scene makes me queasy."

Esther bumped her forehead with the heel of her hand. "I knew it. We should have called. You two needed help."

"No. You did right to leave well enough alone," Colette told them. "The doctors were completely at sea trying to help a queer woman who broke herself posing as normal. They tapped her out for weeks with medications, but at least the drugs tamped down the fires inside her. The doctors prescribed time off, but no, she somehow functioned here; at home she couldn't bear visitors,

TV, or reading the papers. Opera records calmed her, but feeding her—I might as well have thrown water into the wind; it came right back."

Edie said, "Don't you know, Fritzie, you never fail to put on a first-class show right here at the Gold Room? Why do you need a costume or a club act? This stage will always be here for you."

A faux fur cloak slipped from a customer's hands. Fritzie, moving like a ball player scooping up a grounder, caught it. She strolled the room, held her grandfather's Dunhill lighter for a man with a cigarette. Although these were both new patrons, neither looked askance at Fritzie, her tie, or her gentlemanly manner.

The old woman in diamonds and hearing aids, Mrs. Pope, beckoned.

Fritzie, with a damp wink at Colette, Edie, and Esther, made her way over.

The woman loudly asked, "Why is it you waltz only with the youngsters?"

Fritzie helped Mrs. Pope up, signaled to the piano man, danced her around the room and back to her gentleman escort. Then she bowed. Mrs. Pope curtsied, saying, "I didn't approve of a daughter taking over The Gold Room, but you, my dear—you're a fine addition to the menu."

Fritzie made her way back to their table, smiling, a hint of her former jauntiness in her step.

WE WERE A ROOM

Hannah Larrabee

From my mouth comes everything
the shudder of earthquake
the scattering of animals
worship of sunset somewhere
in the rhythmic overlap of fields
I whisper *what do you want*
and note the shadow numbers
of your watch; I am here to overthrow
what you want or maybe you
put my hands around your neck
and lean back into the valley of pillows;
mountains beg for the current
and capture of rivers, what do they want
but to move or outright disappear
they are tired of distorting light
and you might have me by the wrists
but I am summiting
clouds; what words do you have for me
when we are warping in a tintype sky;
then you ask me to return to you
from the place I have been that got you
off this mud-ridden palette;
how many times did I run my hands
up the back of your neck and still
you cannot call me by name
across the table where we redraw
the borders of feeling; tell me
so much you didn't tell me why
did it occur to you in bed that I
was not to spend the night in the way

one spends the day, or spare change,
or a lifetime of study;
if we were a room
and a bed and the moan of that collision
then we were a room
     in the dark we could not find a lamp.

PAINTER

Hannah Larrabee

How many shades of light will it take to consider your eyes,
working mainly with midday sun, two sunrises, and one sunset

on the river that spoke in wind -- then the night: the world behind
your curtains is a world dropped to the floor, your black silk

robe at my feet. I think of Saturn when I think of you: firm in orbit,
sharpness of glistening rock. Cassini took its final plunge

knowing well what we all do: to observe we must lose ourselves.
And I was there for a moment, anyway, in your eyes. I could see

the rings of green, the darker planets. We are fools with names
for colors -- we kiss a hundred ways and most recently in pain.

Have you felt this at the easel, when what you see will not rise
to your hands? I don't know what to do with your eyes. Like birds,

the world they live is kept from me -- and I have walked to the edge
of the Milky Way in just one lonesome evening. On your shoulder,

I traced each light that swept across the wall as you slept, as if that
was the way to ever know you.

FOR ANOTHER HUNDRED MILES
Kelsey Ahlmark

On my drives from Yuma to Tucson I was the sole witness to the changes coming over the desert. I saw how the sunsets to the back of me were somewhere along the shores of the Pacific Ocean, three hundred miles west. In the distance, I could spot the desert storm and where it dropped the dust it picked up and swirled before becoming still again. This happens when the ground temperature changes due to the shadow of a high-rise cumulous rain cloud. Occasionally a car was left stranded on the side of the road. Once a car was on fire. White crosses marked the highway. *Someone had died there,* I thought. Sometimes there were two crosses.

When I used to teach full time, when I was unsure of my place and sexuality, and when I was still trying to become an adult at twenty-four, I would drive along a three-hundred-mile patch of what I now know as part of the Devil's Highway, which actually ran south of I-8 near the Arizona and Mexico border. Its road was paved a total of four lanes that ran from Yuma to smaller-than-Yuma towns like Welton and from there to Gila Bend and from there to my hometown of Tucson. There were two flat lanes west and two even flatter lanes east. On these drives, I was driving east, away from the sunset and away from what I thought were are all my problems. The drive gave me time to think. I could be alone. My job rarely allowed the luxury and my spare time was spent making up for lost sleep, an impossible task scientifically. I made this journey once every month, sometimes twice, for three years.

I loved this highway because of how beautiful it looked at dusk, noon, or just after midnight, which were the only times I ever seemed to be driving it. Yuma was all sand and tumbleweed, except for the manicured yards, which were a vibrant green even in a dry, but mild, sometimes warm winter. This must have been because of the Colorado River's path that was redirected by a man-made dam, lessening the burden and price for water in a desert. Winter in Yuma was a jacket in the morning and at night, but never during the day. Favorable Yuma winters were also the reason why so much of the countries iceberg lettuce was on supermarket shelves in December. It was an agriculture town and its produce was harvested by migrant worker hands and packaged by Dole. What Yuma was not was the high desert of where I was going. Where I was going I could see saguaros. Saguaros did not exist in Yuma. Maybe it was too close to the border of California or maybe because it boasted less rainfall and sunnier days than any other Arizona city, but I didn't start to see them 'til I was about two hundred miles out of it.

I had moved to Yuma to teach high school English in 2010. *But there's no culture there* was something I had heard often when my plans to move became permanent, after finding an apartment and enrolling in my credential program. I wondered if the luxury to move and then find a job was a generational thing or if it had always existed, but I was doing the opposite. This opportunity to teach came during the recession. It was during this same recession that the advice given to college students to major in whatever they wanted changed to major in business or science, not the humanities. I was willing to go anywhere to escape the judgment I gave myself for having a college degree, only to be using it to clean the house of a single doctor four days a week, drive her daughter to school and tennis practice in the evenings that were blazing with heat, and watch their dogs I loved while they were away on long weekend trips out of Tucson, which was something I thought I wanted too at the time.

*

I had rarely seen highway patrol on this route, but I had been pulled over once. It was for speeding, an act I'd been ticketed for several times, but just this once the officer let me go. He shared with me his idea for a novel. I wish I still remembered the conversation, but I did remember his advice: *Don't drive if you're sleepy and call 911 if you need assistance.* His advice reminded me of the good-old-days all of our parents seem to talk about, back when young women like me would go missing and were never found after their cars broke down. It reminded me of the unsolicited advice men gave women about safety. I didn't care that I was alone though. I sometimes had passengers with me, usually other teachers with family or lovers in Tucson. I always drove, not just because I loved the drive, but also because I had command over my car, though not my life. Perhaps that's what I was missing while living there, a sense of control that always seemed so fleeting to me during my mid-twenties as I finally started to seek out independence from my parents.

    The drive out from Yuma had me feeling excited for the possibility of what my life should be. At twenty-something my life could be more carefree than it was years prior. As an undergrad, I thought about how simple life would be once I graduated and had a degree so I could start making my own decisions. But even with those things in place, life had become more complicated especially after I had come out as a queer woman to my parents. On the weekends that my parents had wanted to see me, the drive from Yuma had been marked with anxious thoughts about what my life had come to represent to them. I wasn't the same daughter who asked to be held or told a story to anymore, something I imagined went by too quickly for them. My anxiety fluctuated depending on when and how you would ask what I was feeling. Sometimes it was an excited kind of anxiety. I had ideas. What if on Monday I showed the kids a motivational YouTube video clip and used it to inspire them during the week? Often on my drive home I had bought more things that I didn't need. I had made the purchase as a way to satisfy the desire in me to buy what could be bought and then put away and never used. Other times driving back to Yuma was a relief from escaping my parents as they forbade me from coming home for Thanksgiving or whatever conflict was finding its way into my life because of their intolerance towards my girlfriend. Either feeling was unavoidable. Mostly, I wanted to escape my parents' judgement and the weight I carried from it. Instead I escaped into my mind on the drives and into the seam of a desert horizon. It seemed like the setting sun would last forever, but in reality, forever was fifteen minutes of unaltered bliss, a tie-dyed pillowcase at a sleepover.

*

Because I often drove alone, I talked to myself and convinced myself of things I believed: how much I believed in immigration reform or working in title one schools; how I never wanted to be a teacher, but somehow found myself imitating one for more money than I have ever made before, which is sometimes a salary mocked for its low pay. I wondered if I made a difference to my students (ninety-percent of them Latino) and imagined that somehow my presence mattered there in Yuma. That without me, who would tell the kids about the proposed anchor baby law or show them that having nice things that matter in your early twenties meant sacrifice. *See this car?* I would point to the shiny new vehicle I bought on my own before moving to Yuma. *Do you see a baby seat in the back?* These conversations with myself led me to be defensive on the road and I felt the need to have explanations in my head in case anyone asked about how I felt about the issues that swarmed around me: the immigration, the poverty, the teacher salary, the men I was no longer dating, and the supposed lack of culture where I could look up from my book in a coffee shop and notice for the first time ever that I was the only white woman in the room. However, it was often wasted energy because rarely anyone ever asked about those things.

The straight path of the road helped keep my focus. Most drivers I've spoken to about this drive say that it takes them around four hours, while it only took me three and a half. *You must be flying.* I kept my speed at eighty-one miles per hour thanks to a cruise control button. I was careful to pace myself on these dry roads, which continuously tricked my eyes to believe that water was ahead in a sort of cruel optical illusion for those that hadn't seen water in days. I never stopped to use the bathroom at the fast food chains that swarmed the highway exits. My route allowed me to exit early in Tucson, just hitting the brow of the city's limit and then traveling east to the base of the Catalina Foothills Mountains, but before I could even get there I had to drive.

I left school around 4 p.m. I drove down the hill of 16th Street, passing the town's only Planned Parenthood, back to my apartment for my laundry and suitcase. There were no protesters outside the Planned Parenthood building in the afternoon, but sometimes they were there in the morning. A man held a sign that read, "Abortion stops a beating heart." In my head I asked the man what poverty does. The situation was futile. That particular Planned Parenthood didn't even perform abortions.

In thirty minutes, I would cut through the road that led through Telegraph Pass, a patted mound of dirt leading up to a paved mountain trail. Looking up from the bottom to the top didn't make it easier, but looking down from the top made it look like Mars. Brown hill after brown hill after brown hill and a valley of homes tightly spaced together called civilization, or home base. I had hiked and reached the top twice. It was simultaneously the hardest and easiest thing I have ever done with my body while living there. The path was fewer than five miles, but the incline was steep. Like I did as a child on road trips, I imagined myself climbing to the top, which was easier to imagine than to do. Sometimes Border Patrol was on duty there and other times it was just before the town of Dateland. Rarely was there a line, but occasionally and especially on the weekends the line moved slowly. There were two lines; one for semi-trucks and one for passenger vehicles. I slammed my flat palm onto the steering wheel when vehicles began to navigate between the two lanes, cutting lines as the speed lowered from fifty-five to forty-five to thirty-five to twenty-five miles per hour. Border Patrol seemed to always ask the same questions— are you an American citizen, where are you coming from, where are you going—before waving me through. Once a working dog took interest in my vehicle, but they only asked if I had a dog in the car.

I wished I had a dog in the car. Usually in the back seat of the car was just a hamper of dirty laundry, a weekend duffle bag of clothes, and on occasion, my lion head rabbit Pax, who sat and laid quietly in his travel kennel. Pax was going home to Tucson as well. I bought him one winter from a feed store there. Before I would leave Yuma for good to move further west, I gave him to a nine-year-old girl participating in 4-H. He was a silent car companion and was rarely a nervous passenger even as I sped down the winding road through Telegraph Pass just before reaching Welton.

The tiny town of Welton had one exit sign to the right advertising two gas stations. Welton had its own border patrol and school district, but not much else. It was twenty-nine miles outside of Yuma, but could be passed by without ever noticing. A teacher friend of mine had lived out that way. She had two goats and a dog that she kept tied up outside. There were just some things worth forgetting about on that drive, but like when I learned of the dog's death from a snake bite, I simply could not stop replaying it in my mind.

Mostly on these drives I tried to remember who I was. Sometimes I remembered myself so well. I knew what playlists I would play, how to make myself feel better after a tough week of teenage angst from my students, and I always knew which roads I was taking by memory despite the comfort that my GPS map gave me on the dashboard. Other times, I didn't want to even know myself. I left Yuma because I did not like my choices there— to stay closeted, but maybe more than that, I did not like who I had become there. I didn't feel like myself because I was no longer a person I set out to be. I wanted to be someone admired for making all of life disappointments about my newfound sexuality turn into something that was finally working to prove that just because I was bisexual that I wasn't confused or damaged. I wanted to be someone admired for being out in a conservative town. I wanted to be brave by coming out to those who would never suspect that I was queer because it would mean shattering their stereotypes of what queer meant, but I think most of all I wanted to be admired for who I was becoming away from my parents gaze of and outside of their approval. Instead of being honest about who I was dating and what I wanted in life with my co-workers in Yuma, I had become someone who was easily hurt by the failure to live my life openly queer. I was hiding from the label of bisexual and lesbian, something I hadn't realized I was doing till it started happening. At my job, instead of talking openly about my girlfriend in Tucson, I entertained the idea of going on dates with the male friends and relatives of co-workers until they'd call and I never called back.

*

This desert was a constant line of sand, burning bushes, and scattered-about pieces of trash that appeared white from the road. This scene went on for about a hundred miles more before an oasis of date trees started sprouting up. Farmers, concluding that the Arizona desert was just as dry as their deserts of origin in the Middle East, planted date trees, which looked like a bloated version of palm trees. The date trees flourished as much as they could in the desert. The name of the town became Dateland. Dateland was famous for its thick vanilla ice cream date shakes I never tried. Dates reminded me of prunes and prunes reminded me of relieving constipation. A few rows of trailers and cars in empty lots ran alongside the highway. There was also a deserted playground where a school might have been. I could never imagine teaching there, but I also imagined that someone must and I wondered if that someone was at all like me: a young female, transplanted from the city to a place with nothing but solitude and a long-distance relationship she kept quiet about.

Despite how I felt, the constant was the barren land and sand that continued for another hundred miles. At one time I might have thought that it could have gone on forever until I reached the Sonoran National Desert. The rise of dark rocks with deeply rooted giant saguaros lined the roads and horizon. The loss of cell phone service lasted about twenty miles and would elicit feelings of panic if I was to be left stranded there. A few picnic tables and rest stops served as land markers for those that broke down, but what marked it as a reserved land was the first sight of the sacred saguaros, the first I saw on my journey east. Truly, those saguaros were as sacred as they were rare. They were offered more protection than any other living plant in the state. They stood straight and tall, well over ten feet. They were the color of green beans. Not only were their trunks thick with stored water, so were their long arms, which reached up to where I imagined the Creator lived. In Yuma there were no Saguaros. I had to learn to respect the desert once I moved to one when I was thirteen and again ten years later, but only out of fear of getting left in it alone.

In contrast to the beauty that existed in the desert, there were mummified bodies south of the I-8. And in contrast to the real problems of the world, once while in between Dateland and Gila Bend I became suddenly stricken with the unmistakable feeling of diarrhea. Having no time to make it to the bathroom, I was forced to pull over and shit in a fast-food plastic cup. If you've ever peed in a cup, it's alarming how close the warm urine reaches to the top of the cup and how I might have never known this if I hadn't decided to do such a thing. The same can be said about shit. Rather than throw the cup out immediately, I put the lid on and kept it in the car till I could throw away in Gila Bend. Human waste might be ugly, but much worse is a plastic cup full of human waste on the side of the road. It will sit there and bake into dry solid and then who will pick it up? Since it was my shit, it was my responsibility.

The fear carried me through the recently paved road. The slaughterhouses back in Gila Bend, where cars may have cruised behind or in front of me, exit to highway 85 up to Phoenix. Late at night, when I was driving back to Yuma, several cars drove toward those same slaughterhouses because that is where the driver and its passengers worked. The smell of the slaughter and shit though, they followed me, but with so much rain, the blooms in the desert helped me forget. More than any record in recent memory, saguaros bloomed and released seedlings; some scattered by birds, others devoured. Nature could be cruel like that to its own kind. Perhaps nature was more about survival than it was about kindness.

The ecosystem was greener outside Gila Bend. More water existed there than salt, but still more sand existed there than water. The water moved through untapped sources and the runoff formed lakes and left wounds open that won't heal. As I drove, I was getting closer to where ground water was collected and used for drinking. Where there were pools of water, bird feathers were also on the ground. No matter where I went, I had discovered that if I looked up at the sky and saw a moon when it was light outside, I knew that it must have been the early morning or late afternoon.

Once I reached a close enough cell phone tower, I started making phone calls again to let those expecting me from Yuma know that I was about an hour away. There were only ten more miles of desert solitude until I hit the strip malls, outlets, and fast food parking lots of Casa Grande. I never stopped in Casa Grande. I never let the empty strip mall fool me into thinking that no one ever stopped though. The strip mall existed because they hadn't torn it down, but they built a newer, bigger strip mall on the other side of the highway. The one thing I had learned from that drive was to get it over with as quickly as possible. Unlike Casa Grande, you could be alone for stretches of time completely aware that you aren't supposed to be here. Towns like Casa Grande can fool you into thinking that humans have tamed the desert, but anyone who's been stuck outside on a hot summer day will tell you otherwise.

Outside my car the desert hummed from drought. A monsoon had been waiting to drop. The desert didn't look so recognizable from there. Two lanes east turned into four lanes south straight to the imaginary line that separated the US from Mexico, but only physically. An ostrich farm existed on the right side of the highway with large blue and white signs there to tempt you to feed pellets to the hungry ostrich. Behind the farm was Picacho Peak State Park, with a towering mountain as long as it was high. It resembled a sleeping Dr. Seuss character, the Grinch. Years before I started making this drive, a tiny private plane accidently flew too close to the ostrich farm, causing a stampede. The stampede left many ostriches dead and the ostrich farmer in debt. The ostrich farmer tried to hold the pilot of the plane responsible, but the pilot was cleared of any wrongdoing. The ostrich farmer had deer, goats, and donkeys too. I stopped there once to feed the burros and the goats, which protruded their heads from a wood wall forming a row of live goat heads. They made a real-life wall gang. I wondered where the ostrich bodies were buried in the desert.

After driving some two hundred miles and just outside of Tucson, it began to rain. Something else changed after Casa Grande. I was no longer the only driver. I had to make an effort to watch my speed, to not get carried away by the momentum of having to navigate the lane changes between others driving too fast or too slow. I had to not get carried away by being in a place where home became a loaded word for the first time. The drive swept me up into a storm and dropped me somewhere home used to be, but that I didn't recognize myself in anymore. Home bordered here. I took exit 178A and merged onto I-10. Sometimes I saw a police SUV waiting in the distance for speeding drivers. I passed by un-chased. Maybe that's all

I was ever doing, just passing by the way jellyfish floated out there in the currents of the Pacific Ocean that was six hundred miles away. I was surrounded by the humming desert when I remembered that jellyfish moved only because of the currents that pushed them along. It was called free-swimming.

I was twenty miles away from home. My back was facing the desert sunset, but my eyes hadn't seen the last of it. I wanted to drive for as long as I could without stopping while the rain flooded the river beds. I had been driving for only three hours, but during that time everything in me felt altered, even as the world hummed on.

PERSPECTIVE

s. b. sowbel

I have known you since
your hair was copper
and your form lithe
with confusion

and now when I run
my fingers through
the silver milkweed-silk
of your head and hug
the thicker frame
of your knowledge
I remember

when we were pebbles
nestling in the aggregate
of some tall wall left
by receding waters
to bake and splinter
till we tumbled uncoupling

> yet by dint of some gothic
> unforgetting
> and the long, long
> shadow cast over
> those lithic days

> we have found, again,
> our common rock
> and I sigh, relieved
> that alarming lessons
> of perspective—

    where points vanish
    down the distance
    and all parallels
    disappear—

no longer threaten.

SNOWMELT

s. b. sowbel

Those who study things that change form,
slowly, over time: geologists,
volcanologists, dermatologists,
    hunger for evidence of change.

This is their work.
And now, mine.

I vow to follow their research methods.
I vow to follow their procedures:
    to immerse in study, to attend to detail
    to commit to deep comprehension
This is their version of love and

You will be my study.

The surprise bruise of brown on your wrist.
The softening of your jawline.
The gradual droop of your throat.
The sudden tremor in your hands.
The slow stratifying of your skin.
The drop in your water table.
The stumble in your step.
The explosive release of effluvia.

I vow to observe, document, conjecture, appreciate
and cry as the scientists do when revelations arrive
from previous eras, visible in our earth's striations holding
    events in the minerals of the arctic's cored ice,
      bygone catastrophes in air miles from the occurrence,

your infant self peering from your hooded eyes
like lost car keys shining through snowmelt.

These are my vows
for this late marriage.

FAR FROM THE HIVE

s. b. sowbel

The hidden holds the richest nectar.
These are the blossoms I seek.

Ginger deep under the bent apple tree.
Eastern teaberry down near the beech.
The woman, not ravishingly young

but full ripe and

everywhere.

MOTHER

Nora Beck

THE BUGGY ONES

Timea Gulisio

The stag-beetle is my favorite animal, if I can call it that way, which every time I catch it, I put it in a bottle filled with chloroform, then I stab on a needle. I have a full collection of them and other insects, since there's never enough.

On an early summer day I was at Fuckey's, we were droolingly looking at a commercial magazine, especially at the special section about drinks. The untimely arrived heatwave was choking me, and the constant dampness of the dark apartment didn't help. I stepped to the rickety and bony window and I opened it with a big crackling.

- Don't! The light is hurting my eyes, I got unused to it! - whined my old girlfriend.

I closed it, but for some reason it didn't close entirely. That something has cracked too. It was a big male stag-beetle, which was scrolling slowly with his broken back-half on the ledge. Naturally, I could not resist grabbing it and put it under Fuckey's nose in order to frighten her, as I did to my grandmother.

- Ouch, my little Timi, what's that? How pretty! - clashed her hands together.

I should have known, that a medic is not that skittish.

- What comes in your mind about him? - I asked, though I knew it for sure that it didn't come the same as in mine.

- My childhood. We found one like this, we tied a thread on its leg and we flew it. Poor thing.

- Don't you remember something else?

- I do, the God, the genesis.

Here I thought it was better to interrupt her, before she didn't get in a holy mood.

- Would you allow me to put him in your palm?

- I would – she replied after a short hesitation.

We tired it, too. She was trembling, but she held him. He climbed up her thin and venous arm. She had goosebumps, but she didn't throw him away. He went until her neck, where he was half way in the collar of her dress.

- He's such a bug as his owner – she pointed at me blushing – he wants to "bosomize" me.

I freed her from him, but I didn't put it far, just to the other side of the bed.

- Would you undress me? - with this I instantly began to free her from her black spangly upper, and also from her black leggings.

She sit naked in front of me, with crossed legs, and with a veil-like look. The bug got closer to her pillow, but he didn't bother her. I grabbed him in my hands, by his back carefully, far from his horns which he ferociously clattered together. I held him to Fuckey's thigh, so that he almost touch it, not quite. Some kind of strange horniness stood in her eyes.

- You're sick, my child! - she whispered, but in this situation she was the sicker one, it was not me who got horny from the six-legged monster.

She was trembling and was nervously wobbling with her legs, as if she'd like to have sex, but is afraid to initiate. I put the bug on her thigh. She screamed with a gurgle, like a girl on the beach, when the boys sprinkle her. She waited with a heaving, for him to climb upper, she laid lower, in order to make climbing easier for him. He reached her tits which were dangling on her belly. She adjusted him on her nipple.

- Take that, suck!

It was a dangerous stunt, he could even bit it down, but she arranged it so that it got in between the gap of his in-bending horns.

- What ideas you have, you girl! - she shook her head.

- This specifically wasn't my idea – I lied, although it was exactly how I imagined, but she found out herself, too.

- Should I put him somewhere else, hmm? - she asked waggishly, and she put it.

He was stumbling holding on to her pussy-hair. This was much for me too, that place is mine.

- Enough! - I shouted at her, but she stared back at me with her moo-cow eyes.
- Now comes the rest of it, Hey!
- Just don't say that...
- I'm not saying, I'm doing it! Wouldn't you believe the things I did when I was your age! We even stuck up the components of the skeleton from the tool-house! But, in those days they weren't made out of plastic! Here's one in the shed.
- You used to do it with that?
- Nooo, since it's a she!
- Does it matter what kind the skeleton it is? And so, I'm a girl too.

This latest statement of mine was acknowledged with a usual wave of her hand.

Meanwhile the victim has crawled down on her leg and rested on her foot, just on a good and most sensitive place.

- So, I was in everything in which I could possibly be in, and everything was in me.
- And everyone – me completing the sentence.
- This is natural – she said, and with a vain movement smoothing her gray tonsure – If you could have seen what a woman I was!
- Or (me) too ! - I slammed the possibility of the compliment down, since I got quite horny because of something, or of her, or of the skeleton story, or of the beetle or of all of these together.

I put the newcomer on her collarbone, then I washed my hands. When I came back, she was petting herself in full swing, she didn't turn a hair that her hand was not clean. She was masturbating with open mouth and stuck eyes. I watched from the armchair. The cattle climbed to the top of her head, then he opened his wings and flew around the room. I kneed in front of my sex-granny, and

I licked her navel. She was pulling her nipples. On one was visible the trace of the gripping of the horns of the beetle. She put a pillow behind her back, she was leaning on it, because she could hold herself hardly. She hanged one of her leg on the handrail of the armchair. I kissed in her withered rose, but she pushed away my head.

- We have a buggy day today, don't we? Where is it?
- There on the curtain.
- Bring it to me, if I may ask!

I stood on a chair, and I tried to exert his legs from the laces of the curtain.

- Would you take off your clothes, to watch you meanwhile?

I threw off my easy summer stuff, and climbed back naked on the chair. I sweated until I got him.

- Please! - Fuckey reached her hand to me.
- No, he is mine!
- You got the feel, what?
- No, I collect bugs.
- And what do you do with them, where do you keep them?
- In a box, in nice order.
- What do you feed them?
- Poisoned cotton wool, and pin.

This is when she realized what I'm talking about.

- Don't kill him, give him to me, I need... So, don't hurt him, he has his own life here on Earth.
- So you need him? - I caught on her word.

At this time she dropped huge tears, maybe because of the humiliation, maybe because of the new plaything she had lost.

I've put him in a plastic bag, then in my big snappy wallet.

- Here he can be safe, he can't escape. He remains forever, or at least for many years. He'll be at me, and when I feel my end is near, I'll hand him down to the local Museum of Natural History. Many thousands will see him, until museum beetles will eat him up, little by little, and it won't hurt him anymore.

- You convinced me, for sure! I want to be a bug, your bug! - she hugged me, we kissed, then without the actual sex, but we happily fell asleep.

A buzzing woke me up, luckily it was just a fly, which came to drink the tears from the corner of my beloved one's eye.

EMERGENCY ROOM IN THE DESERT

Patty Willis

Are you with me
as I wait for news?
Could your holy pen
cross out some parts
that I don't like
that are coming too soon
for all the plans I have
laid for the world?

I didn't know that
in the middle of the desert
You had built a hospital with
flashing emergency room signs
but when I make it inside
out of breath
already forgetting where I parked my car,
You don't come out to the reception
to receive me.
There are only chairs screaming:

Sit down and wait!

Wait, not sleep,
for the arms prevent turning the
row of chairs into a bed.
The floor too dicey to consider.
Posters everywhere with
magnified photographs of infections
that could be found here,
Superbugs that can take off

arms might not be attached to the bottom
of my shoes.

Wash hands now!

Even the arms of the chair
are for elbows not hands that could
carry microscopic destroying forces
through the air and into the nose
or mouth or ear.
This waiting is hard even when
I see these hours as the culmination
of the journey,
the complex penultimate scene when
happiness is out of sight
around the corner
waiting, too,
as movie stars wait in their trailers
near the set
sipping drinks
as they practice their lines
trying not to think that each mistake
could cost thousands in ruined film.
The cost of caterers alone for one day
could break the bank.

Fear is not helpful
and a vending machine
sells Swiss chocolates
so fresh there is no turning back!
I buy two and save one for later,
feeling, as dairy milk melts on
my tongue and slides back to my

taste buds stealthily spreading bliss,
that this could be all there is.

Satisfied at last with
that red faux leather chair,
the heavens open and shower
meteors too small to cause damage
like rain that hold sparks of light:
You.

Emergency Room in the Desert

PSALM AT FINISTERRE

Patty Willis

When I speak with the dying
I am standing at Finisterre,
the long road behind me
the certificate of pilgrimage
in my backpack,
the sea ahead.

People close to dying
rarely speak.
Their lips are moving
not to form words
only as a sign of life:
I am here!
For two more hours,
minutes,
sometimes days pass,
lips moving as babes asleep,
the beginnings of dreams,
images forming not from experience,
touching something else.

Knowing much about the roads
traveled in their mother's bodies:
vibration from cobblestones,
the exertion of steep inclines,
the relaxation of wide open grassy spaces,
the slowed heartbeat of sleep.

At death, the body reveals
the Earth, a hovering womb,

the air thick around a deathbed
like heavy blankets holding
limbs in place.
Sometimes the dying struggle to the surface
like children born under water
remembering at last the backstroke of
ancestors who made their way to land
crossing species
finally
returning to air
as dinosaurs with wings,
their traces
captured in ancient ponds.

When paleontologists,
excited at the new find
linking life to sky,
work into the night brushing off
layers of sediment
revealing mouths and feet
the delicate bones of wings,

they too stand in this place
the end of the Earth
looking out at the sea
for schools of mackerel
near the surface
silver flutters
glimpses of skin over thick tasty flesh.

I stand on the edge
watching.
Death has a timing of its own
an hour,

a day.
When I pray around the dying
I tell them they can go.

Their lips move.
Sometimes eyes open
then look away.
May the love you brought to this Earth
Be a cloak for your journey.
A pilgrim's staff.

PSALM AT A TIME OF MOURNING

Patty Willis

I do not like Death. Is she your sister?
The sibling who hides in the back room
afraid of the light.

I didn't invite her
and here she is,
hardly a knock on the door
before she appeared in my living room
taking up too much space on the couch,
not touching the tea and cookies I laid out
hoping to please her.

And she, refusing to take my hints
that it was time for her to return home.
Now!

I see her steely resolve.
She will not change her mind.

I prefer the days when I didn't hear her at all
or when her sound from the depths of the house
was so slight,
I thought, "Mouse."

Now, she lives everywhere.

The other day, I found her
in my bathtub, soaking up to her neck
In bubbles from a bottle I had never opened
under the sink, labeled "Cherry Blossoms."

Was she hinting that I should
find her beauty
as samurais did
drinking sake before a battle,
under a tree in full bloom,
blossoms falling everywhere
like weightless soldiers
dying a good death?

I prepared a fluffy towel and held it out
bidding her to rise
and together we sat
in the chair large enough for two
a trail of petals all the way to my study,
evidence that soon would be gone.

I felt comfort.
Her body,
imprinted in that place
below my heart,
installed a lock box containing all the data
about the Mystery
of disappearance as sudden as an airplane
above enemy land.

I, like the family of the victims,
will pay anything for a bit of debris,
a memento.

It is all there, Death whispered,
her voice surprisingly sweet.

They say a shaft of light will lead to Heaven.
but how can I believe
those who have returned?

Could that light unlock the box I will carry
always, like old buttons slid into
my praying hands?

Spirit of Life, is Death your sister?
Ask her why she has become so silent.
Tell her that a room is waiting
in the back of my house.

COWARD BEING

Sarah Yasuda

Cicadas have an emotion-intense, time sensitive life. Nearly, if not completely, most of their life is devoted to searching for their mate. In comparison, I was ashamed of my lethargic self, for not acting immediately, for not pursuing that person I've wanted to be so close to. I stopped myself in fear of the consequences that would follow if I were to go through with it. I feared disgracing the expected.

You can hear the cicadas screaming, echoing in mass numbers as each individual scream intensifies into a pulsating sea of crashes and recessions. It's too overwhelming when logistically thinking of the number of cicadas actually surrounding the trees I pass by. As Tokyo's summer nears its end, they're expelling all they've got within that cruel space of time before they fall onto the ground and turn chalk white.

I let the record finish its rounds as I drifted off to sleep last night. The last I remember was Nico's *These Days* playing and being enwrapped in a blanket. I woke up to a brightly lit room, the record still left on the turntable, and my paint brushes dried up, scattered on the coffee table. The curtains welcomed enough light to warm up the hardwood floors. I sat on the bed feeling no urgency to hurry off as I would on a work day.

Blankly, I sat on my bed. Then something warm and dense trickled down inside of me. It oozed out. I felt the liquid spread and sink itself into my sheets. *Shit. My period.* I hurried off into the bathroom and sat there for a little while. There's a medium that I enter when it comes to periods. Part of me understands that this comes in a routine manner, it's natural. But the other part of me is shocked; a small spark of anxiety ignites in me enough to feel for a moment that I'm going to die. Within this narrow opening between life and death, I roamed, half asleep, on a Saturday.

It was noon. In an effort to organize my time so as not to be late for dinner with some friends in the evening, I saved enough time to read at a cafe.

I stood up, naked. The cat came up to me and looked up. I felt ashamed and embarrassed. I was ashamed for being ashamed – as the cat, with no capacity to understand what being naked meant, stared back at my exposed body. My sense of self seemed to diminish slowly under the guise of the cat's intense, judging gaze. I scooped a cup of rice from the kitchen. With the rice cooker on the floor, I crouched down and dumped the grains into the metal bowl along with some water. I pushed a button and a tacky, high-pitched jingle followed – the rice should be ready within an hour.

I took a shower and drowned out the loose strands of hairs and thoughts. *Why did I feel so vulnerable in front of the cat? Isn't my vulnerability stemming from my ability to get dressed rather than my nakedness?*

The jingle, as if with more confidence since soundcheck, perforated the entire parameter of my apartment and most likely to my neighbors' to let me know that the rice was ready. Grabbing my *chawan* (rice bowl) and pulling out the poorly wrapped container of kimchee out of the fridge, I winced at the sour, pungent smell wafting inside the refrigerator among the milk carton, fermented soybean packs, and salad dressing bottles. The aging kimchee was stinking up the place. I quickly dressed myself, the black cotton dress hanging a bit damp over my body and left.

There's a cafe with anime characters drawn all over the walls. It's a two minute walk from my apartment. The coffee is a bit expensive, but I like the sparse amount of people there. The guy also plays pretty good indie bands. I went in, the guy glanced, and gave me a sharp nod to acknowledge my usual presence on a weekend afternoon.

I brought Judith Butler's *Gender Trouble: Feminism and the Subversion of Identity*. The last thing I underlined with a dulled out pencil was, *There is no gender identity behind the expressions of gender; that identity is performatively constituted by the very "expressions" that are said to be its results.*

I was sipping my cup as I heard the doors of the cafe swing open. In comes an old man with pudgy, sagged-out cheeks. He's mumbling things under his breath and takes a seat two tables away to my right. A few moments later, a petite-sized woman comes hurrying in. She looked frantic, and plopped in the chair across from the man. The laxity of the man's response was painted with disinterest. I felt an unsettling feeling that made me want to flee.

Something dense was twisting and turning in my lower abdomen. I arched my back and bent over – I hunched and continued sipping. The pain was progressively getting worse.

"He never replied to my message," said the old woman.

"You have to stop bothering him like that," the old man continued to look through the menu.

"He could've at least left a voicemail. I get nothing from him, nothing."

"He doesn't have time for us anymore and – ."

"Do you know what he said the last time we talked on the phone? That he wished we died already. He wants us gone."

"Nothing can be done."

The woman twisted her mouth to one side and an exasperated exhale followed. The two sat there defeated.

Wittig refers to "sex" as a mark that is somehow applied by an institutionalized heterosexuality, a mark that can be erased or obfuscated through practices that effectively contest that institution...

"We're becoming too much of a burden."

"Remember when he cried for hours because I left the house to run errands and you had to look over him? He couldn't even sleep without holding my finger at night."

"Now he's just waiting."

"No, the curtains have already drawn long ago."

"We don't belong anymore."
"Where should we go?"
One is not born a woman, but rather becomes one.
"What are we, now that we've outgrown what we've been becoming all this time?"
"I guess we wait."
"Oh no, we're half an hour late for the lunch set deal."

I wiped off the lipstick stain that encompassed the brim of the tea cup, tucked my book under my arm, and got up. The station was damp with a smell of old, sweaty socks and drenched t-shirts. I browsed through my phone. One hand clenched to the metal steel bar protruding vertically from the floor of the train car and the other hand, my cell phone. A warm vibration took my hand by surprise, I nearly dropped it.

"Meet @ West gate."

We decided on a Turkish restaurant in Shinjuku. Yumi's supposed to be there, along with the usual group. The train car picked up more and more people with every stop. Finally arriving at Shinjuku, I inched myself a step closer to the person in front of me, waiting for the doors to slide open. I felt the guy behind me move closer. I thought he was going to bite my neck and grab me.

We spilled out and trickled down the stairs. Shinjuku station is nausea taken for the worse after one too many drinks mixed with a 'bad trip'. I maneuver through the crowd the best way I can but sometimes you can't help but take it personally when you're in a bad mood. I had to change my pad soon. It felt heavy, and the flood of people expunged onto the underground walkways did far from helping me feel distracted.

I looked for my train card among the mess of keys, mass clusters of unwanted flyers (I got 8 different flyers just after going to one gig, ONE gig!), an abnormally long wallet, and tubes of makeup. I tapped out of the station gates, luckily finding the right exit before my compulsion to exit whatever one closest to me out of claustrophobic exhaustion took a hold of me.

The Turkish place sat right between a British pub full of expats and a ramen shop. Right by the station, the tracks ran parallel to the places that lined up neatly like irregular Tetris pieces.

I was the last one to arrive, but it's been an overly played out gag that stopped being funny by the fifth time I was late meeting up with them. They've accepted my unintentional tardiness nonetheless. We met at more of a takeout place, seating optional. It eerily reminded me of the deli sandwich place back in the states. I ordered a basic wrap and went upstairs to the table where all my friends gathered.

We talked about something, but I was completely out of it. I had absolutely no interest, kind of like being submerged in water, I heard muffles of things but the fluids filled my ears, preoccupying my interest.

"I feel like my back is just hardening into a shell, sitting at my desk all day." Yumi scoffed as she said it, I felt a little sad.

They really stuffed the meat in the wrap. It was falling out as I stuffed my face into the opening, heading face first into the bloom of Turkish meats and shredded cabbages. We still had about an hour before a band was playing nearby at a small bar. We took our time, ordered some beers and headed out.

"So it's supposed to be some band touring from Germany, I heard they're really fun." I was walking next to Yumi. Her blond bob was cut short at her chin with her bangs right above her eyebrows. The black cotton shirt was a bit big on her, but it fit her look. Yumi was small, but had presence in her voice.

We got to Fume Kaneko, a small bar filled with a decently-sized library in the back. The name, I'm assuming, came from the Japanese anarchist, Fumiko Kaneko. It's not just the overt resemblance of her name but in addition, the types of books they kept - a collection of anarchist books and not surprisingly, classic nihilistic works crammed quietly in the corner.

The band already started playing. I got a gin and tonic and tried getting closer to the front. The bar was only able to hold about 70 or so people max and it was packed. By then, my cramps went somewhere. That wet, gushy feeling was still there, but it seemed that the music asserted itself in place of my sharp abdominal twists and turns. The music drowned me, close enough that I nearly went deaf for a moment but I felt submerged in it. As I swayed, Yumi and I looked at each other and smiled. It was a certain kind of look she gave that made me feel completely exposed and vulnerable. I felt so open with what felt like really no sense or grasp of the moment. But then I reached a point where I felt paralyzed.

I wanted to step outside for a bit and smoke. I imagined Yumi and I sitting outside on the curb. It was a Saturday – something could happen. Immediately, thoughts flushed into my head. It was thick fluid that made it difficult for me to follow through with my actions.

All of a sudden Michel Foucalt, the French philosopher in his iconic leather jacket and white turtle neck, appeared before me and said:

> the notion of 'sex' made it possible to group together, in an artificial unity, anatomical elements, biological functions, conducts, sensations, and pleasures, and it enabled one to make use of this fictitious unity as a causal principle, an omnipresent meaning: sex was thus able to function as a unique signifier and as a universal signified...

He then kissed my forehead and disappeared into thin air. I then felt something vibrating from my back pocket.

"What time are you gonna be here?" He messaged me. It was nearing midnight and I had to leave before the last train. As chemicals made me feel afloat, emotional exigencies spiking high, confusion deterring my own autonomy, I was in a state of flux. I rushed out and I caught a glimpse of Yumi turn her head my way.

Defeated, I crammed myself along with the other commuters. He looked startled when I tried crawling into bed, but he was also glad I was home. He then went on top of me and started kissing my neck. As I lied there, my fingers moved the curtains slightly and I saw the rain pouring hard, creating little puddles in his balcony.

The weather report expects continuous rain for the next couple of weeks. I saw a chalk-white cicada on the floor of his apartment lobby.

FEVER

Deborah Miranda

for the house, and the spirits, at 203 S. Randolph St.

1.
I'm thinking of you tonight, Diego
and Jane Evans. Twilight eases over
my shoulders like an indigo cloak;
I walk past the two-over-two brick house
you built in the late 1840s – complete

with basement kitchen. Did the two of you
sit on that porch of a June evening, watch fireflies
play slow hide and seek over the graves
of the adjacent cemetery? It isn't famous
yet – Stonewall Jackson's headstone

is still granite inside a mountain, uncut;
Jackson himself tours New York,
visits Niagara Falls, reports for court
martial duty at Fort Ontario. You, Diego –
Black and free, successful merchant,

study law: Lexington isn't big enough
for you, your children, your dreams.
Do you see it coming, Jane – Civil War?
Your children's freedom fickle as lightning.
Colonization is the answer: to segregation,

discrimination, life confined on the Black
side of a small Southern town. You sell
your beautiful house on South Randolph

Street. Emigrate. You need a whole country,
one with a name you can ring like a bell.

You will settle for nothing less.

2.
List of Emigrants by the Liberia Packet, Capt. Howe, from Norfolk, Va., January 26, 1850, for Monrovia and Bassa, Liberia:

No. 107 Diego Evans. 39. Trader. Reads. Free.
No. 108 Jane, his wife. 30. Reads. Free.
No. 109 James H. F. 8. Reads. Free.
No. 110 Richard P. 7. Reads. Free.
No. 111 Lavinia Ann. 5. Free.
No. 112 John. 4. Free.

3.
Some interesting services were held at Lexington, Va.,
on the occasion of the departure of the emigrants

from that county. Our correspondent says,
"We had a farewell meeting on their account

on Wednesday the 19th in the Presbyterian
Church, which called a large audience. Col. Smith

of the Military Institute, and Rev. Dr. Junkin, President
of Washington College, addressed the congregation

in effective speeches on colonization; Maj. Preston
addressed the emigrants in very appropriate terms.

They were seated together on the right of the pulpit.
The Rev. W.S. White also addressed the meeting,

and led in prayer. Original hymns composed
for the occasion were sung; first by the people

led by the choir, and last by the emigrants.
The whole services were impressive,

and, I believe, of good effect for the cause."
signed, Miss Margaret Junkin.

4.
...Not poor and empty-handed,
    as first to us they came,
With superstition branded,
    And want and woe and shame, --
Are we the race returning
    Back to their native sod,
But with our laws – our learning –
    Our freedom – and our God!

5.
Mary J. Henry, daughter of John V. Henry, writes
to friends in Lexington, "We rented a house on Broad

Street and Diego rented a house on the water side,
which all the old settlers told him not, but

he thought he could live there – being a good place
to sell his goods. But all his family took the fever.

We took the children home and they all got better,
but Diego and his wife departed this life."

6.
Ours may be a lot of trials,
  Bravely we will meet them all,
For the sake of our dear children,
  We will bear what may befall.

Dear Virginia! Dear Virginia!
Loved, Oh loved, whe'er we roam,
Dear Virginia, loved Virginia!
Farewell – farewell, dear old home.

7.
Liberia is like a fever, Diego;
colonization a contagion, Jane —
spread by fear of free Black
bodies walking unchained
through a white world,

a virus stoked by The Fugitive
Slave Act's long arm a shadow
behind those bought or born free.
Frederick Douglass rails against
this "return" to Mother Africa,

fearing mass deportations —
Jane, do you watch your sons
and daughter sleep at night
in this house, await that loud
knock at the door? I wonder,

Diego, what is the difference
between Liberia and a reservation?

"Let us buy you a country,"
the American Colonization Society says,
" —sorry, sorry, for all that slavery mess —"

what they really mean: slavery
for you is safety for us;
your freedom, our worst
nightmare. They set this fever
on you, squeeze so hard

you have no place else to go.
Colonization is contagious.
Liberia is like
a fever. Catch it,
or be caught.

ALBUQUERQUE

Deborah Miranda

This is not a poem about late-term abortion.
This is not a poem about crossing state lines.
This is not a poem about failed birth control.
This is not a poem about desperation or denial.

This is a poem about the chance recessive gene
that changes everything. A poem about a toddler
who cannot walk, speak, feed herself, say *mama*.
This is a poem about seizures, brain trauma.

This is a poem about orphan drugs costing $40,000
a week, about days full of waiting rooms, PT,
OT; a poem about sleep deprivation. This is a poem
about pain writing a love letter to the future.

This is not a poem about patriarchal law.
About protestors with anatomical posters and bullhorns.
About poor health care for poor women.
This is not a poem about police with guns inside the clinic.

This is a poem about donated frequent flyer miles,
prayers, beds and food given in grace;
about the silence of kinship between women
in a run-down hotel with a clinic discount.

This is about riding in a van with tinted windows,
Kleenex shared with strangers. This is a poem
about the pearl of kindness inside a dead-end maze,
unwrapping the ways we are still human.

Against all odds, to my surprise,
this is a poem about gratitude.

THINGS FIRE CAN'T DESTROY

Deborah Miranda

Burn letters, books,
bridges. Burn down
a courthouse,
a church, a forest.
The human body
stores it all: the pistol of grief.
Fist of lust. Facts
of abandonment.
Wonder of scars.

Burn the body, then:
immerse it in fire. Use
the flamethrowers
of suicide: cocaine,
heroin, starvation.
Use tools of genocide:
Small pox, ovens.

In theory, if you burn
enough bodies, you can
incinerate memory.
Burn enough memories—
you can rewrite history.

In practice, memory lives on
in subterranean streams,
deep veins cut channels
into the next hidden spring.
Memory seeps like an oasis
waiting to wet the parched

throats of truthtellers
who go on, nesting one
inside the other,
like an egg inside
a lotus
inside
a phoenix.

VENICE BEACH

Deborah Miranda

Turtle Woman wants bare feet on sand that goes on for miles,
hair whipped into knots by wind. She wants salt, bits of ancient

mountains between her teeth, old hand-painted VW vans
in parking lots, curtains made from thin beach towels.

She wants tattoos of dolphins and mermaids; Muscle Beach's
strut and sweat, battle cries of seagulls, low fog blurring

waves. Turtle Woman wants to walk past decades of loss,
past erasure. She wants to walk so far, so long that she walks

right around the spiral of history, back into that black and white
snapshot taken in 1962: her first wobbly steps on this beach,

where blue water baptized her into a tribe, named her
with a blood-sister vow. Turtle Woman wants the smell

of exile scratched off her skin, wants to smell like ocean,
like history. Like home.

OFFERINGS

Deborah Miranda

At dawn the songs begin again as if never sung before,
as if the jet stream has not wandered from its path,

the Arctic ice shelf does not melt at accelerated rates,
Sudden Oak Death does not leapfrog across the continent;

Shenandoah Valley songbirds lean into the indigo air
as if two thousand snow geese did not fall from the sky

in Idaho, ten thousand sea lions are not washing up dead
in the Channel Islands, train tanker cars full of chemicals

never crashed into the Kanawah River in West Virginia.
As if California's Central Valley agriculture is not pumping

twenty-thousand-year-old water out of ancient aquifers
that cannot be refilled. These song warriors pitch morning

as if the territorial prayers of robins keep bee colony collapse
disorder at bay, as if crows stitch each torn morning together

with their black beaks, mockingbirds know the secret
combination of notes that command God's ear, the low *coo*

of mourning doves weaves feathery medicine; they persist
as if pine warblers, flash of gold in treetops, coax the sun

up by degrees, as if these musical beings don't know the word
extinction, as if, knowing it, their silvered melodies insist

like the yellow warbler: *sweet-sweet-sweet; little-more-sweet.*

THE TIDE

Anastazia Schmid

The tide pulling you out further than
you've ever been
Taking you into the depths of
esoteric utopia--
    washed back to the beginning of the lullaby
Caress dark primordial wetness
Fear not what gives you your breath

Held in the arms of creation
    this is all there is
Suspended
    the 'tween:
Being and not being
Activated, animated,
    captive, still

Open the crease
Reveal the flower and the iris
This ocean blue that reflects
Your soul
No solitude in Oneness
No return

The tide pulling me out further than I've ever been.

CRESCENT WATER

Sara Koppel

MARY AND THE MERMAID

Meghan Bell

Working on her father's fishing boat suited Mary just fine. There wasn't much to do on most days — her father ran a charter company, and the boat was usually populated with two to four sleepy tourists whose poles she would set up an average of three times each per trip. It was like clockwork to Mary, and that wasn't why she came.

She came because she loved the sea. The chilly mist parting as the sun peeked out over the long horizon was the highlight of her days. Feeling the sea spray on her face as the bow skimmed over icy water could beat a cup of coffee every time.

"Fish on!" she would hear, five, or six, or eight times a day, pulling her from her reverie and the little paradise at the bow. Today she would have no time for daydreaming. She ran back and forth, dropping lines into the deep and pulling fish out of the water for a grinning couple in matching windbreakers and their quiet, bleary preteen. When she finally got a chance to rest, she had to sit down — even her seasoned sea legs were about to give out. She sank into the ratty cushion of the bench inside the cabin. There was just enough room in the tiny cabin for what she had always assumed was a re-purposed diner booth, a cabinet full of teabags and instant coffee mixes (regular and decaf), and a tank that dispensed both hot and cold water.

She sipped on a glass of cold water and wiped at beads of sweat pooling on her forehead. The air was icy outside, and the cabin windows fogged over. She wiped at the starboard window and peered out at the choppy waves.

The waves peered back.

Mary spat out the last sip of her water. The spray coated the window, clearing it of fog, and Mary could see quite clearly a pair of very human-looking eyes staring at her from just beneath the ocean's surface. Mary stood up so quickly it made her dizzy. She stumbled, and when she regained her footing, the eyes had disappeared.

I'm seeing things, she thought. She stepped out of the cabin, cautiously. She checked on the tourists, counting their beanie-clad heads – *one, two, three*.... She peered back into the cabin, where her father sat in the cockpit, smoking his old pipe that he thought made him look like an old sailor. She shook her head. *I'm imagining things.*

Mary wasn't the type to imagine things. What she loved most about working on the boat was that it was always the same. The sea may rock to a different beat from one day to the next, and no two sunrises were quite alike, but the basics never changed.

"Fish on!" One of the tourists let out a giddy laugh.

"Mary!" her father yelled from the cabin.

"Yeah!" she yelled back. Like clockwork. Pull the fish on board, drop the line again. She headed to the narrow length of walkway along the starboard side.

Mary crouched down. She hung on the railing, pulling herself forward. She searched the dark waters for a sign of anything, but no – just darkness. She bit her lip, frowning.

She didn't wait long. The flick of a tail, the glint of a green scale flashed before her eyes. The tail was long, and flat like a dolphin – but a dolphin's skin was smooth and grey. Dolphins would swim next to the boat sometimes, playfully racing them as they made their way to deeper waters. This was no dolphin.

The eyes emerged again, and Mary's heart nearly stopped. For a moment they just stared at each other, Mary's eyes wide, the ones beneath the surface of the water blinking idly. Then Mary opened her mouth, as though to scream or call for help. The face below the water tilted upward, and a finger rose to its mouth, shushing her.

Mary's mouth snapped shut. She was still crouched low on the deck, and her legs were beginning to cramp. She knelt, water, salty and freezing, soaking her jeans in seconds, but she was transfixed by the slow-blinking eyes of the creature in the water.

"What are you?" she whispered, and slowly reached a hand over the side. Her fingers trailed the surface. A hand came up to meet hers. The touch of the creature was electric – Mary had half expected to feel a piece of kelp, given life only by her lack of sleep. She was surprised at the warmth of the creature's touch. She pulled her hand back, clutching at the rails.

The eyes disappeared again, but before Mary could let out her breath, the creature shot through the dark surface of the water. Its hands grasped at the railing where Mary's had been moments before. She fell back, gasping. A woman's face, tinged with green, stared at her. Dangling from her torso was the long, green tail.

"Definitely not a dolphin," Mary breathed. The woman laughed, and it rang in Mary's ears like church bells. "Did I say that out loud?" she said, mostly to herself. She didn't know how much the woman could understand her.

"Yes," said the woman. *Oh*, Mary thought. *That much.*

"What are you?" Mary asked again.

"What do you think?" asked the woman. Her voice was like listening to a seashell. It echoed in Mary's head.

"A mermaid," Mary said, shaking her head. "But you're --" *Real.* The word died on her lips. The woman looked at her expectantly.

"I'm waiting." The mermaid smirked. Her skin, despite the green glint, had not felt slimy or cold. Her lips were pleasantly pinkish, and her eyes, once outside the surface of the water, shone silvery-blue.

Mary's face flushed. "You're beautiful," she said.

"I know," said the mermaid. She ran a hand through her long hair, shaking free a strand of tangled seaweed.

"Fish on!" The voice of one of the tourists came faintly from the stern. It seemed worlds away. Her dad's voice rang indistinctly in response.

"You're welcome," said the mermaid, smirking again.

"You're helping us catch fish?" Mary asked, puzzled.

The mermaid appeared to be growing bored with her questions. "Well," she said, "If you don't want my help I'll leave you to it." She let go of the railing with one hand and turned as though to jump back into the sea.

"Wait!" Mary shouted, then stopped, not wanting her father to hear lest he come running. "Wait," she said, more quietly this time. "What is your name?"

The mermaid seemed amused, but slightly peeved. "We're not like you."

Mary didn't know what to say to that. "Well," she said slowly, "What should I call you?"

"What would you like to call me?"

She thought for a moment. "I'd like to call you Serena."

The mermaid giggled. "So cliché. But all right. What should I call you?"

"My name is Mary." Mary felt suddenly self-conscious. Serena was a perfectly good name for a mermaid, she thought. At least she hadn't gone with Ariel.

"Nice to meet you, Mary," said Serena.

Her father's voice rose above the surf again, calling her back to the deck. Mary stood up and bit her lip.

"You'd better get back to work." The mermaid smirked at her once more.

"Will I see you again?" Mary asked.

"You won't tell anyone, will you?" said Serena. She put her finger to her lips again. *Shh.*

Mary shook her head emphatically. "No way my dad would believe me."

"Good." Serena turned her head toward the sea. "I gotta get going. But yeah, sure, you'll see me again." She winked, and with a flash of green scales and a quick *splash*, she was gone.

Mary scurried back to the fishing deck. Her father raised an eyebrow.

"Where you been? Got three fish on at once, and we had to let one of 'em go."

"Sorry," Mary shrugged, trying not to make eye contact. She wasn't too good at lying to her father. "I was in the head," she said. Not terribly convincing, considering she had just come from the side of the boat, and the toilet was in the cabin. She smiled weakly.

"Alright," her father said. His eyebrows were nearly disappearing behind the brim of his yellow fishing hat, but he didn't question her further. "Drop a line for Mrs. Murphy, will you?"

Mary nodded and got to work fixing the broken line on Mrs. Murphy's pole.

"Lot of fish biting today," her father said, heading back into the cabin.

"Yeah," Mary nodded. She turned to the starboard side of the ship. "Thanks," she whispered. The glint of green scales flashed in the corner of her eye, and bell-like laughter echoed in her head.

WHERE DID OUR LOVE GO

Mariposa

A tale of lesbian love
One cannot conceive of two more disparate and contradictory people than my lover and myself. Erica Kaufman, the subject of this story, is white and of Jewish ancestry, I am Puerto Rican and loosely Catholic. Erica is very intelligent and graduated from one of the most prestigious universities in the United States. I am a high school reject. It wasn't so much that I dropped out as I was pushed out by the stupid rules and boring classes. Erica had been brought up on Fifth Avenue, living in a condominium that her family owned. I am a child of the projects. She had gone to a series of exclusive girl schools, culminating in Barnard College where she majored in Film Studies and minored in social activism, she dressed to the nine's when she wanted to, and possessed a certain elegance impossible to capture in words. She had curly brown hair, black eyes, stood five foot tall and didn't have an ounce of fat on her body. If she had had the talent, she could have been a dancer, with the Julliard or some other institution. And, in the beginning, when we first got to know each other, she was straight, at least as far as I knew.

My name is Esperanza Canales. I weigh less than one hundred pounds, stand in at four foot six inches, am dark skinned, have wild and crazy curly hair, I have a quick temper and, when I was young, was just as quick with my fists, even with the boys in my junior high school, JHS 149. I guess I had a biological father, but I never knew him. I was the oldest of four children, with two sisters and a brother younger than me. My mother worked in the Garment District until the jobs all went south and raised us kids with no man in her life.

The neighborhood I was brought up in, El Barrio or Spanish Harlem, had been plagued since time immemorial with street gangs and all the vices that they brought with them. I had lost my virginity when I was thirteen, to an older uncle, a gang member. The asshole came into the bedroom I shared with my sisters, shoved me down on the bed, told me to get undressed, and then without further warning, put his gross hairy body on top of mine, began to grunt, shoved his penis inside me, and then came. I screamed in agony and he slapped me across my face and warned me not to mention this to anyone. The experience so nauseated me that I swore I would never have anything to do with men ever again. I had gone to a series of public schools until I was expelled for truancy when I was fifteen and that was the end of my academic career, at least for a long while. I became a small scale pot dealer which was common in my neighborhood at that time. I mainly dealt to other kids from my junior high school who had gone on to high school. I always had good quality stuff and kept my prices reasonable. It brought some much needed income into the house. My mother wondered where it came from, but didn't question me too closely.

"Mi hijita, I just hope you aren't selling your body like some puta in the streets. You should know by now that men are devils and cannot be trusted. Let some man get into your pants, he'll get you pregnant and when you have the baby, he will be nowhere to be found."

"No, mom, I am not a hooker. And I don't rob banks either. The cops don't care about what I am doing, so you shouldn't worry either. As soon as I get a job, I'll stop dealing." There, the cat was out of the bag. My mother turned pale and began muttering to herself in Spanish, about where she had gone wrong.

I told her "Mom, you haven't done anything wrong. That SOB who was my father who deserted you, this lousy welfare system that keeps us confined to the projects, the poverty that we live in, they are the reasons that maybe I'm not an ideal daughter, but I'm not going to do anything that would bring shame on the family. I love all of you too much to do that."

I eventually moved out and moved to the Lower East Side. For about two years I had a lover there, but then we separated. I met Erica at a teach-in on abortion, but didn't stay in touch.

As I wrote earlier, we came from two very different and divergent backgrounds. I don't need to repeat all that I wrote earlier, but I think it is worth saying that, in the normal course of life, we would have never met. We were divided by race, class, education and background. But we did have in common the fact that we were both women and by the time we became friends, both of us were dedicated to the women's liberation movement. That may not seem like much, but it was enough to cement a life-long relationship which continues to this day.

I was selling our women's liberation newspaper one day in Washington Square Park and a woman came over and said "Esperanza, is that you?" For a minute I didn't recognize her and then I remembered the teach in on abortion way back when. She had been there for that. If the teach in had been in 1969, then a decade had passed, since it was now 1979.

"Yes, I'm Esperanza. You're Erica, right?"

"Right. Are you really busy? I'd like to but you some coffee or something."

"Sure, that would be great. What about the McDonalds down by Sixth Avenue?"

"What about if I treat and we go to café Reggio? They have great espresso and some good food too."

I took her up on her offer and we went down to the café she had mentioned. We settled in at one of the booths they had in the back of the café and began talking.

"So, I see you are still politically active. I'm in graduate school at the New School, majoring in cinema production. Since I saw you last, I discovered that I have a real talent for making movies. I was involved in a radical film making project in Mexico, but we were all expelled from the country and the film never made it to the big screen. But the experience whetted my appetite for cinema, revolutionary cinema to be precise. I hope I can use my master's to land a job with a radical director or producer, especially if the project involves women's issues. I'm still a radical feminist. So, what about yourself?"

"How do you sum up a decade? Well, I've been in nearly every radical feminist group in New York City and in several groups that were strictly for lesbians. I don't know if you knew this, but back in the late 60s and early 70s I had a lesbian lover. But I haven't seen her since 1971. I've had a couple of lovers since then, but nothing permanent. I work for the women's newspaper you saw me selling, both as a writer and a street seller. From time to time I also go to meetings of one of the groups that survived the carnage of the 60s, Redstockings. I'm pretty close to them politically, but I'm not a member. There are some points where we don't see eye to eye. Nothing serious, but the group is serious and wants total commitment from its members. So, right now, organizationally, I don't belong to any group. Some of the male left groups tried to recruit me, but I have no use for them and told them so. So, in their eyes, I'm some kind of counter-revolutionary, I guess. I did go back to school, got my GED and spent some time at City College, but the whole academic scene just isn't for me. My mother is still alive and living in the same apartment in the projects where I was brought up, but all my sisters and my brother have flown the coop. They did a lot better than I did. They got their high school diploma and went onto college and even graduated. I guess you could say that I'm the black sheep of the family."

Erica responded "You know not all education can be found in those academic buildings that alienated you so much. The professors don't have a monopoly on education. There are places we can learn and people that we can learn from that have nothing to do with formal education. For example, let me ask you, you've been a feminist for a decade now. How much reading have you done on the women's liberation movement, either from the time of the suffragettes or the modern day movement? There is a lot of great history there of importance to all women."

"I pretty much have stuck with the newspapers and pamphlets that the various groups have put out over the years. I liked the Redstockings Manifesto because it was so clear and went right to the point: the idea that men are the oppressor class and women are the oppressed class. I read the declaration by the Radicalesbians that came out in 1970 and agreed with it. And I liked Robin Morgan's piece in the liberated Rat. But that is as about as far as my reading has gone. I was always more of an activist than an intellectual. So, the answer to your question is that I really don't know that much about the classic or the new women's liberation. I guess I could learn, if had a teacher, but the women at the newspaper work on it full time and I've lost touch with a lot of the women I knew back in the days."

Erica responded "Well, let me ask you something. Do you have a place to live right now or are you still doing the whole crash pad scene?"

"I share an apartment with some other women but might be interested in moving. We aren't a collective or anything, just roommates. Why do you ask?"

"Well, if you want to know the truth, after my experience in Mexico I also came out as a lesbian, but right now I am living by myself in a one-and-a-half-bedroom apartment. I remember the passion that you brought to the movement back in the beginning, I'm impressed that you are still a part of it (so many aren't) and I would be honored to be your teacher in feminism. If you move in with me, we could spend a lot of time reading together, discussing ideas, seeing how they relate to our scene today and so on. I could use a lot of your street savvy in my work in cinema so you could teach me and I could teach you. I've never had a friend who came from a background like yours. I'm sorry to say that my life has been surrounded by other white intellectuals of the upper class. You would be like a breath of fresh air for me."

I think I understood that there was an implicit part of this arrangement, that we might go from being teacher and student, activist and thinker, to being lovers. And since I hadn't had a real lover since 1971, the idea intrigued me. I was intrigued by the idea of the two of us, so different, coming together and forging something new (I learned much later that this is an example of what is called the Hegelian dialectic, that through the opposition of a thesis and antithesis, the clash of the two, a new and higher synthesis will result). I had no real connection with the women that I was living with, it was a month to month rental, so I thought for a while, had another cup of espresso, and then, with a big smile on my face said "You've got a deal roomie."

I didn't own a lot of stuff, so Erica and I went to the apartment and moved me. My roommates were okay about the move so there were no issues there. I told them that I would spread the word at the newspaper that there was an apartment looking for a woman to rent a room in. So, everything was cool.

Erica also lived in the East Village. She had a railroad flat, with a large room in the front, two small rooms in the center, and a combination of kitchen, bathroom, and dining room in the rear. We put all my stuff in the middle room and I rolled out my sleeping bag for my bed.

"Now, that is absolute nonsense. I have a perfectly good bed in the front room and you are very welcome to share it with me."

I didn't have to be asked twice. My body and soul ached from the lack of a serious relationship all during the 1970s. I still mourned my first lover, Yo, but with Erica in the picture, I decided that it was time to move on. So I walked over to her and wrapped my arms around her. She returned the embrace and all of a sudden her tongue was in my mouth. We kissed deeply and then, having rapidly undressed, fell into bed. I was in heaven. Finally, after all these years, I had a woman who was not (I felt this in my heart) a passing thing, but a woman that would love me and whom I would love until, as the saying goes, we would be parted by death.

From that point on we were voracious lovers. That is what I meant when I wrote earlier that she was my professor in the art of love. But along with love, we shared a commitment to the feminist revolution.

"The more I make love, the more I want to make revolution; the more I make revolution, the more I want to make love."

That could have been Erica and I's slogan as we entered into the 1980s. She taught me everything that I had never learned about the suffragette generation, the women that had won the vote for women, and what we now called "the second wave" of the women's liberation movement. I read De Beauvoir, Friedan, Shulie Firestone (I had known her but never read her book), and Mary Daly. I read the socialist feminists, the Marxist feminists, and the lesbian separatist feminists. Then Erica discovered that there was a Women's Study department at the City University of New York. She pushed me to apply, I did so, and within a year I was majoring in women's studies, hoping to get a degree, hoping to teach. I'd come a long way from being a high school push-out, pot dealing, East Village lesbian. Erica and I survived the Reagan years, the defeat of the ERA, the rollback in women's services and the waning of the second wave feminist movement. But we never lost faith and we never lost hope. Erica went on to become an independent movie director in New York City, specializing in films by women and about women. I was given a teaching position at an independent girl's high school, where my lesbianism was never an issue. I had a satisfying thirty year career as a teacher and then retired. We built up a large enough library that we had to move to a two bedroom apartment, with one bedroom for us and one for our books. We joined the computer age and then the Facebook generation. We joined Older Lesbians Organizing for Change (OLOC) and matured, grey hair and all. Best of all, we never fell out of love with each other.

I guess that about wraps it up. Maybe if I drank another mug of coffee I could write another dozen pages, but I'm under doctor's orders to drink one mug a day and no more. And I love and respect my doctor so that is what I'm going to do. I just hope that this memoir had helped you understand better how a Puerto Rican girl from El Barrio found true love in the most unexpected place, with the most unexpected person, and how I embraced my destiny as a lesbian and a revolutionary.

PURGATORY

Jade Homa

we tried to staple ourselves
together,

painfully and without
remorse.

most nights, we spent so
much energy trying to
make it work
that we forgot how to
love.

we never fit like puzzle pieces.
our bodies never met.

but oh how we tried.

- we broke apart so we could live
and not just exist as office supplies

PILLOW TALK

Bec Ehlers

I spend most days pretending this body isn't mine.
    I kneel on the floor, letting the sensation leave my legs; I lean on my arm til it falls asleep. There's a moment before the sharp pricks of pain when I can focus in and feel like my limbs are floating away without me.
    I wait for the breaths when I don't have to own this. In the shower when I don't look down; I sing tenor, all the parts I want to play and never will. When I'm first waking up, flat on my back, and if I don't move I can see myself in a smear. Shoulder to thigh, like someone scrubbed an eraser in up and down strokes.
    The checker calls me "Miss." My employer has no idea. A man on the street screams, "Suck my cock, bitch!" and somewhere in the fear I note that he thinks I'm a woman.
    She's the first one who saw me, really. Asked all the right questions. Delicately turned words around her tongue until she found ones that slipped onto me like a worn sweatshirt. The kind she steals from my closet and brings back smelling like her hair.
    She sees me even on the bad days. On the bad days I wrap myself in memories of being six and telling people I was half-boy, half-girl until I believed it. Pelvic exams with more shame than I could comprehend. Every time I have stood in front of the mirror pulling my breasts taut until they ache, weighing their warmth in my hands against one more reason for someone to doubt.
    But when the bad days come I think of the way her eyes glowed when she stroked my cheek, kissed my breast as I lowered myself onto her, and whispered, "My gorgeous boy."
    I think of the way I pressed my forehead to hers and felt twenty-three years trembling, and how she murmured over and over, "My gorgeous boy. My gorgeous boy."

BOOK REVIEWS

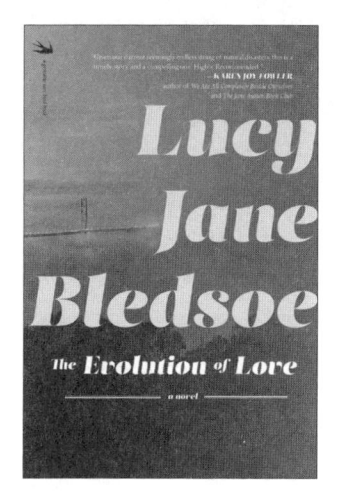

Evolution of Love
by **Lucy Jane Bledsoe**
Rare Birds Books, 2018
Paperback, 302 pages; $16.95

Reviewed by Roberta Arnold

Lucy Jane Bledsoe creates a landscape of characters and ideas that ignite both heart and mind in *Evolution of Love*. The premise of the book came from Beldsoe's research of the Bonobo Apes who share 99% of their DNA with humans—and may soon be extinct because of man's inhumanity to man, earth, and animals—and who solve problems by utilizing love and sex in matriarchal dominant and female bonding groups. Lily, the central character, creates a discourse of love and compassion in relationship to these ancestors. Lily is on a mission to rescue her older sister in the aftermath of a cataclysmic Bay Area earthquake. The two sisters are opposite in many ways: Lily, the younger, stayed in Nebraska with an unimaginative husband and did seasonal gardening work. Vickie, the lesbian character, not knowing how to interact within society's constructs but able to do algorithms in her head, left Nebraska to find challenging work. I saw Vickie as the allegorical lesbian persona: life threatened by social restraint and machismo violence, brain forging a path to rise above.

When Lily lands in San Francisco, she goes directly into the disaster zone. As aftershocks rock the earth, Lily grapples with the meaning of love. "See that was the problem with love. It slipped out of all the ordinary parameters... Was it possible that love truly existed, maybe more than any other thing? But how could something that couldn't be measured be real? Here was a new idea: maybe love couldn't be measured or quantified, but it could succeed if you followed certain regulations" (168).

Lily's compassionate, measured response understands others through observing, listening, and looking past external indicators. When volunteering to serve community suppers, Lily meets Annie, a biracial girl who demands an extra milk for her friend, Binky, the gay man-child she protects with large loyal presence. Although Annie's tone and demeanor are gruff and hostile, Lily perceives the vulnerable core. "Annie did a good imitation of a gangster girl, but, really you only had to look a second longer to see that she was just a child. Her long eyelashes fluttered against sorrow, and the dimple at the side of her mouth twitched with fear" (111). Annie butts up against Lily more than once before becoming a crucial ally.

Kalisha, Lily's boss at the church, is the first person that Lily meets in the broken Bay Area landscape. Kalisha's story is intricate and layered. We see the hierarchy of shame society builds upon people in prison: a friend who admired Kalisha when she was on her way to getting a master's degree, then locks out their friendship when she is in prison. Looking back on that day, alienation and shame steep through Kalisha's thoughts like a bitter drink. "The worst memory of her life was the day Mrs. Vernadsky had come to see her in prison. Her gray hair in that messy pixie cut, the penetrating gray eyes, the full mouth that loved to smirk, all transformed into a tableau of confusion. Kalisha saw how she struggled for compassion but felt something more like outrage. She shifted in her chair on the other side of the table as if she could hardly sit still with her disappointment.... For her, the waste of a mind was the greatest failing" (141). Despite the austere past, or perhaps because of that, I saw Kalisha as the most complex and judicious person in the book. She becomes a figurative leader/ teacher by action and deed, making sure that people who need help have a fair chance at survival.

Lily, the eternal learner, takes notes, writing down the salient points on love and evolution: "That's the whole thing about evolution. It's the most exciting narrative of all because it's about change over time. Real change. Change that sticks. Change that improves the odds for the changed. Change that increases the intricacy of our dependence on one or another" (232). As Lily navigates the crumbling world around her, she witnesses firsthand how the notion of natural selection has become outdated and why the misinterpretation of "survival of the fittest" leads people to violence and destruction. "The thing is, when people think of evolution, they think of creatures battling it out for survival. That's not what Darwin meant by "survival of the fittest." What if natural selection favors altruism? What if love improves our chances of survival? Maybe love and survival are the same thing! I don't know what love is. I don't think anyone does. But maybe our human descendants will evolve there, to an understanding of love" (233).

The most disturbing example of "battling it out for survival" comes when Lily's sister, Vicky, is viciously attacked after trying to help one of the survival clusters—a group ironically led by the man who taught Lily about the Bonobos and their compassion in pen-pal letters she received from the Congo. One of these letters becomes something of a prophecy: "What if, in the long, long run, the warlike people tear each other to pieces and are less successful at reproduction? And the people who have learned to cooperate and make peace are in fact more successful at carrying on?" (160).

This was a hypothesis I first heard spoken by my mother in the early seventies, when lesbians, women, and African Americans first began to work toward liberation together—in a world intent on annihilating them, the cooperation didn't last. We are at a similar tipping point in history where aggression challenges our survival. In this adventuresome story, fulfillment comes on so many levels. Told in multiple flowing voices, this is storybook adventure of the best kind: where adventure, political meaning, beauty and truth create the best happy-ending message. Throughout this stunning read, my heart and mind blazed and popped like a crackling hearth.

Chapter Eleven
By **E.F. Schraeder**
Partisan Press
Paperback, 36 pages, $10.00

Review by Sara Gregory

Chapter Eleven is poet and scholar E.F. Schraeder's powerful indictment of capitalism, class, and undervalued labor. As a professor, Schraeder was highly educated and woefully underemployed. She holds a Ph.D in applied ethics and for over a decade worked as an adjunct professor. During that ten year span, Schraeder went uninsured, even as she dealt with serious health issues. Through her own experience, Schraeder exposes a healthcare system and work culture that leaves poor people behind.

"The Policy Writer" was one of the most striking poems in *Chapter Eleven*. Schraeder confronts the normalization of unethical work policies. Observing how policies transform insensitivity into "sympathy," Schraeder writes:

> The Company also respects your right to illness,/ so with that in mind, your first sick day deducts/ automatically from your paid vacation accrual...Then take as much time from the 1 day earned/ every 30 days with a maximum of 5 per year you need./Feel better (6).

Ranging from punitive policies to family life *Chapter Eleven*, weaves a complicated story of interlocking disenfranchisement. Debt-ridden college students, struggling families, "uninsured, part time brains," and the "masters of secondhand cool" all find voice in *Chapter Eleven*. Perhaps, Schraeder muses, the only way for her subjects will retire in America is to "exploit advantages/stake your claim in a shrinking pie./ Prey" (16).

Chapter Eleven is a poignant, if rightfully disillusioned, collection made stronger by Schraeder's wry, exacting style.

So Lucky
by **Nicola Griffith**
Farrar, Strauss, and Giroux
180 pages; $15.00

Reviewed by Roberta Arnold

In *So Lucky*, the protagonist, Mara Tagarelli, loses her job as Executive Director of the Georgia AIDS Project and the physical control she once had over her body in the same week the neurologist said: "It's Multiple Sclerosis," (p 9). The week before her wife walked out. Her life is forever changed. She is told to rest. For exercise: try Yoga. Mara thinks, "Yoga. Chanting crystals and good will to all men. I'd rather hit things." (11). The triple whammy sets off a declaration of attack against age-old patriarchal belief systems and the fight is worthy of a feminist supershero.

"*Victim. Sufferer.*" Like a mantra, the two words ignite a fire in Mara. She takes careful notes: how people perceive her, how the words people use around her change, and how her own physical reality changes with disability. Griffith's ability to bring the reader into the moment is unsurpassed. Every new treatment, every needle stick, every fall, and every thought, I feel with immediacy and power. Humor catapults with the perfect timing of stand-up comedy. When Mara is writing up the budget because no one else is likely to get to it soon enough, she taps her anger into the keys. "I was too busy stabbing at the keys and cursing the screen. *Fuck you.* Sum. *Fuck you.* Average. *And the horse you rode in on.* Total. My head throbbed with the engine of a freighter battling a storm." (25).

After she sends the board members the budget by Excel spreadsheet, Mara settles back to take a sip of her tea. Minutes later, she hears her assistant curse. He comes over and highlights on her computer a line of the document she sent. "Where it should have been labeled *Maintenance/Improvements* and *Miscellaneous* it read FUCK YOU and AND THE HORSE YOU RODE IN ON." (26).

Clever humor and spirited pique are interspersed with skillful descriptors that shine a light on the world of MS, at once insightful, penetrating, and welcome: "It's a strange thing to feel a body you know change inside without moving, a kind of shrinking away, like the sides of a cooling cake." (29).

The formal martial arts training in the dōjō Mara knows and loves acts as an incentive to the fight of living with MS, her new opponent. The martial arts skills Mara had acquired in her younger female life, now transformed. "I was fearless until I was twenty-two; until one night in a bar I was beaten by two men and I learned the story that most women already knew: that men beat women for no other reason than they could, because they were raised on the story that women are weak. *We* were taught we are weak. The message was beamed at all of us, from all sides, from TV and radio, plays and movies, novels and jokes, comics and social media: we are weak, we must rely on the kindness of strangers, call forth a man's better nature, placate the savage beast. That night in the bar I understood on a visceral level what I had only known as a statistic: that women's fear was a marketable commodity. Fear sells." (45).

The fear Mara experiences with MS takes on different shapes, form, and consciousness. It invades her peripheral vision, her dreams, and the shadows. She finds a kitten for companionship after going through the process of looking to adopt with the same sharp wit woven like the slivers of a looking glass throughout the novel. The kitten provides more than companionship, becoming something of a role model. "I CALLED HER MIZ RIP, because she looked like fudge ripple and she ripped up everything that got in her way, including me." (47).

Rage fuels and builds. When Mara takes to twitter with her rage, I find myself cheering *right-on!*--igneous rock in my throat, a light turned on in my heart. I am taken back to my disabled days and my electric scooter named Rascal; head swarming with heated energy, a mad whorl of intensity pushing thoughts and feelings. I am thrilled when Mara owns the word, "Crip." Like an outlaw band. I am the crowd of one cheering for the crowd of many as Mara sleuths out murder with calculations of mathematical precision, leaving other notorious sleuths like Margaret Rutherford as Miss Marple, and Sherlock, in the dust.

Suspenseful, and fiercely fast-paced, with a flinty, keenly clever, and funny protagonist, *So Lucky* is a critique of patriarchal society--and a gift for feminists, Crip community, and mystery lovers. I hated for it to end and am looking forward to reading it again. If you have not read the book yet, you are *So Lucky*.

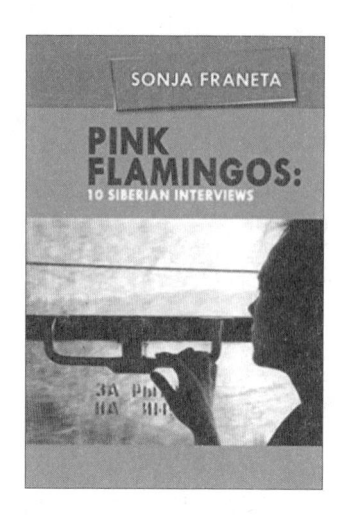

Pink Flamingos:
10 Siberian Interviews
by **Sonja Franeta**
Dacha Books, 2017
Paperback, 161 pages, $9.99

Reviewed by Sara Gregory

*P*ink Flamingos is an insightful collection of interviews between Sonja Franeta and a dozen LGBTQ Siberians. Each interview spans worries, relationships, love, identity development, and the coming out anxieties intelligible to most LGBTQ people. But *Pink Flamingos* is also distinctly Siberian, markedly less accessible (and more interesting) to an American audience because of vast cultural differences. The people of *Pink Flamingos* are deeply affected by the USSR, prison camps, severe housing shortages, and Article 121. Post World War II, the suppression of gay and lesbian life was often even more severe in the USSR than in the United States. Spanning interrogations, coercion, camps, and psychiatric wards, Article 121 was instituted by the Stalin regime and outlawed sodomy. Countless gay men were convicted under Article 121 and sent to prison. Though lesbianism was not illegal under Article 121, women were also persecuted, charged with other offenses, and sent to psychiatric wards. The conversations in *Pink Flamingos* are often fearful, sometimes reluctantly given, even during the 90s, a time of relative openness and security for LGBTQ Siberians. Article 121 was overturned in '93, but but Putin's Russia has since spearheaded anti-gay laws and the suppression of gay life. Published in the Russian in 2004, *Pink Flamingos* offer a unique moment of hope during our current time of heightened international tensions. By uplifting the idiosynctatic as universal, Franeta accomplishes a rare book of optimism, freedom, and isolation.

"The interviews are stories in themselves," writes Franeta, and her 'characters' are varied. Masha and Sonja live in a one-room dormitory with Masha's two children. Masha is bisexual and Sonja is a trans man; both doubt sexual minorities (a term commonly used by both Franeta and the interviewees) will ever be more than outcasts in Siberia. Later, Franeta speaks with a lesbian named Tanya often connected with other sexual minorities "completely by accident," once finding a book by Sappho in an acquaintance's house (pg. 59). Twenty-two year old Martina is a motorcycle-loving lesbian, who disguised as man married her girlfriend in front of an entire village. Perhaps Franeta's favorites, Asya and Lena had a romance that "made them glow." They call each other sister in public, share "slurpy kisses" on the Trans-Siberian Railroad and break up in less than a year (pg. 149).

One of the most striking interviews was with Igor, a gay and lesbian rights organizer born in '51. Igor explained the trails under Article 121 starting in the early 80s:

> As far as I know, we had six big trials, where 130 people were convicted...Along with the 130 who were convicted, many more people were brought to see the trials, those who had escaped sentencing, including me. I wriggled out of it because they declared me insane (73).

Igor regularly cruised a well-known square and was picked up on suspicion of gay activity. In anticipation of persecution, Igor had already been to the regional psychiatrist, admitted he was gay, underwent a ten-day observation to confirm his homosexuality, and at the police station would coolly refer the police to his doctor. During the trials, Igor was declared officially 'mentally ill' but "absolutely...never thought I had any kind of psychological problems" (75). Igor's story is a dizzying reminder that the strides LGBTQ activism has achieved are not universal. But the way Igor, and all of the people interviewed, manage to manipulate the system and avoid imprisonment, find housing (where it often takes ten years to secure a one-room dorm), and even get married is thrilling to read. Sonja Franeta's *Pink Flamingos* is a case study of human ingenuity, a document of unrealized liberation, and above all a testament to LGBTQ optimism.

In Search of Pure Lust
by **Lise Weil**
She Writes Press, 2018
Paperback, $16.95, 367 pages

Reviewed by Roberta Arnold

In the early days of second wave feminism, desire was alive everywhere: desire for knowledge, for freedom from oppression, for lesbian community, for lesbians. Weil meets this desire in 1977: "I was twenty-six, back in graduate school and I was a lesbian. A dyke" (39). Weil's desire takes off with fiery energy amid readings of many great lesbian writers of that time. Reminiscent of the isle of Lesbos, where Sappho's teachings include lyrical outpourings of desire and heartbreak, Weil's journey follows a similar tidal pull--but instead of a Greek island, we find lesbian venues. New York City bars like Bonnie & Clyde's, The Duchess--and Peg's Place in San Francisco, provide a written record for places now gone; the concerts of Holly Near and Cris Williamson thankfully continue.

Weil moves from Providence, graduate school, and her first lover, to a writing group in upstate New York. Sexual awakening leads her through non-monogamous channels, and this leads her to delve further into writing. The writing group upstate with all its non-monogamous bonding leaves Weil put out. She moves to Leverett, a picturesque Massachusetts Mill town, and into in a farmhouse owned by Mary Daly. The magnanimous beauty of surrounding land and the woman who lives in the farmhouse meet all Weil's needs. Together they host a study group with other women, reading and sharing ideas inspired by writings and teachings they love—their community will of love pumping strong. In Boston, attending a feminist conference to address racial and class divides, Weil eagerly shares what she has learned from her study group--from the likes of Audre Lorde, Alice Walker, and in the words of Adrienne Rich: "our dream of a common language." Instead of a common language, Weil meets anger and outrage: the powerful voices of oppression: race, class, and ableism. Weil's pride cries silently. "In the eyes of my Reaganite relatives in Santa Fe I'm a loser, and by the time the conference is over it's hard not to feel the same way here. The only thing I have going for me is the identity I spent twenty-five years trying to suppress. But my lesbian credits are undercut by my white skin, my able body, and my privileged background. Having a Jewish father might account for something—but an assimilated, mildly anti-Semitic Jewish father?"(90). Different voices of identity spin through Weil's experience of conflict in the women's movement. At times farcical, and at times unapologetic, Weil brings us into the center of conflict with lovers and the lesbian community. In a voice alternating between self-deprecatory and irreverent, to lyrical and scholarly, she confronts the discord and her own foibles.

In 1982, she moves from Leverett to Montague, Massachusetts, and begins cataloguing ideas generated by the study group into a publication: *Trivia: A Journal of Ideas*. The title, she notes, came together from Daly's *Gyn/Ecology*: "we had learned that one of the Triple Goddesses had been 'Trivia'—She Whose Face Points in Three Directions.... We would reclaim the word by making it the title of a journal of serious thought by and for women" (145). *Trivia: The Journal of Ideas* coincided with a Feminist Lecture Series hosted and sponsored by Smith College and continued until 1992. In 2005, Weil relaunched Trivia as an online magazine called: *Trivia: Voices of Feminism* which continued to stoke the fires of feminist thought until 2011.

Having moved to the same town as the co-founders of *Sinister Wisdom*, Weil and a *Trivia* co-founder named Anne, come face to face with the rewards of feminist sisterhood. Catherine Nicholson and Harriet Ellenberger, *Sinister Wisdom* co-founders and editors from 1976 to 1981, were getting ready to pass the journal forward to Adrienne Rich and Michelle Cliff. In keeping with the *Sinister Wisdom* tradition of inclusive sisterhood, Nicholson and Ellenberger invite Weil and Anne over for apple pie--in order to pass on what they had to give and what they had learned. "In their sun-lit kitchen over slices of Catherine's deep dish apple pie, they lavished us with advice and encouragement. Harriet offered to serve as production advisor for the first issue. They still had most of their paste-up equipment and would gladly put it at our disposal. When Anne and I drove away we felt we were being borne along on the wings of feminist sisterhood" (156).

Stories like these stand on their own. Like un-earthed turquoise in different colors, sizes, and textures linked together on a single strand. Attending the First National Lesbian Conference in Atlanta Weil follows a woman through the woods to a lesbian sex cabaret: *The Salon Méchant*—the wicked show. There Weil renews her vigor and inspiration in feminism by just having fun. The show starts with a Gregorian chant and ends in a bawdy strip that has all the dykes in the room up on stage dancing together, everyone having a blast. Weil finds herself reflecting once again on movement divisions—this time around pornography and sexuality--and finds herself changing her own viewpoint: "This is fun, uproarious fun! Why did we ever get so worked up about this sort of thing? It's hard to remember now.... What were we afraid of losing? Only everything we believed in, were fighting for. Desire as a force for political change. Desiring out of the wholeness of our being. Did we have any idea how tall that order was?" (302).

All this fun leads to another migration; this one outside the United States. Following gypsy prophecies to another continent, Weil lands in Canada with two cats and a connection to a women's bookstore, L'Essentielle, co-founded by Harriet Ellenberger. In Montreal, Weil meets women who like to dress up and have fun—political fault lines no longer seem to be looming large. French language itself was a familiar bliss Weil had shared as a child with her father. As her father's health begins to decline, Weil steps further into his shoes; she has already begun referring to herself at times in male gender as a prince. Yet the romantic tragedy of Sappho still resonates. "The tyranny of desire. What a wild card it was, wayward and unpredictable. It reared its head when I was feeling wary; estranged—abused even. It flagged when I was kindest and most trusting. It trumped love, over and over again" (330).

Sheer creative energy, spirituality, and survival drive the quest for pure lust to its bedrock. What began as a quest for desire--as the spark point to creativity, spirals around to this ultimate truth: lesbian creativity comes along with protecting our survival. Weil illuminates this in final reflections. "From our desire for women all other desires flowed: above all, the desire for a world where women would not be marginal but central, in which all life on earth would be honored, protected. From Lesbian Desire flowed not only the desire for such a world but the energy to bring it into being" (351).

Weil's journey charts waters at times serene, at times giddying--the boat veering close to menacing rock, dangerous channels—

yet continually immersed in the teachings of our foremothers; the many brilliant writers conjoined in feminist passageway. Weil's peripatetic tale takes us from place to place, unflagging lesbian community branching out from our deepest roots. "We are still women looking out on the world together. When something wondrous happens—or horrific—we will always witness it together, no matter what" (151). Weil navigates us through a consummate Sapphic Odyssey—it is a journey you will not want to miss.

CONTRIBUTORS

Kelsey Rea Ahlmark is an educator, artist, and writer with a MFA in writing from the University of San Francisco and a BA in creative writing from the University of Arizona. She's a fan of the non-fiction essay, true crime shows, western landscapes, veganism, and rescue dogs. Her work explores themes of the southwest desert, home, real and imagined borders, and the female queer experience, and has appeared in newspapers and literary publications such as the *Ignatian* and *Switchback*.

Nora Beck is a musicologist, specializing in the relationship between music and visual art in the Italian Renaissance. She studied painting in Italy with Antonio Postacchini. A writer of lesbian fiction, Nora published *Cauliflower Head* under her pen name, Alison Castelli. Her art focuses on the interplay between motion and emotion. She continues to fight for LGBTQIA equality in Italy: her court case asking Italy to recognize same-sex adoptions reached the Italian Supreme Court in 2016.

Meghan Bell is an author and student living in Portland, Oregon with her girlfriend Carly, along with her emotional support cat, Midnight Monster. Originally from Northern California, she moved to Oregon in 2014. Meghan has studied politics, American Sign Language, and hopes to continue her education studying creative writing. Her work has been published in *RFD Magazine* and *NonBinary Review*. This story is a reworking of one of Meghan's earliest writing endeavors. Interested readers can follow her on Twitter at @meghanelaine.

Michelle Elizabeth Brown is a public speaker, author and activist. Born and raised in Detroit, Michigan she has been a guest lecturer in the role of artist/activist at universities, various pride celebrations, and social justice forums. She contributes regularly to Between the Lines Newspaper, hosts a national weekly internet radio show "Collections by Michelle Brown" and has written two books of poetry *Wild Fruit Hidden in Open Spaces* and *3 Layers and a Brassiere* and a children's book *Jack with the Curly Tail: Home is Where the Heart Is*.

Kinnery Chaparrel is a white disabled autistic low-income lesbian in her mid-twenties. She was born in Meadow Lake, Saskatchewan, and raised throughout Ontario. At the mercy of her mental and physical health, Kinnery occasionally studies at the University of Guelph, working toward a BAH in English with minors in Classics and Creative Writing. She lives with her cat Sylvia in Guelph, Ontario, Canada. Kinnery humbly acknowledges the Attawandaron/Neutral Peoples on whose historical land she resides.

Kai Coggin is a former Houston Teacher of the Year turned poet, author, and teaching artist living in the valley of a small mountain in Hot Springs National Park, AR. She holds a BA in English, Poetry, and Creative Writing from Texas A & M University. Her work has been published or is forthcoming in *Sinister Wisdom*, *Assaracus*, *Elephant Journal*, *Yes Poetry*, *Calamus Journal*, *Lavender Review*, *Split This Rock*, *The Rise Up Review*, *Luna Luna*, *Blue Heron Review*, and elsewhere. Coggin is the author of two full-length collections, *Periscope Heart* (Swimming with Elephants, 2014) and *Wingspan* (Golden Dragonfly Press, 2016), as well as a spoken word album called *Silhouette* (2017). Her third full-length collection *Incandescent* is forthcoming from Sibling Rivalry Press in 2019. Kai's poetry has been nominated three times for The Pushcart Prize, as well as Bettering American Poetry 2015, and Best of the Net 2016 and 2018. Kai teaches an adult creative writing class called Words & Wine at Emergent Arts. She is also a teaching artist on the Arkansas Arts Council's Arts in Education Roster and with Arkansas Learning Through the Arts (ALTTA), specializing in bringing poetry and creative writing to youth around the state. For more information, www.kaicoggin.com.

Caitlin Crowley is a film and darkroom photographer based out of Fort Wayne, Indiana. Caitlin graduated from the University of Saint Francis with a degree in Studio Art. Caitlin specializes in medium format film, preferring the Mamiya camera family. In addition to making photographs, she also writes about photography. "Photography for Students and Artists", a technical and creative photography guide, was awarded an Addy for publication design. Previously published in F-Stop Magazine and Feature Shoot.

Bec Ehlers is a Seattleite turned New Yorker writer and theatre maker with an interest in accessibility and a disregard for gender. They are a proud graduate of Northwestern University's creative writing major, with a concentration in creative nonfiction. Their work has previously been published through Harmony Ink and produced by A Contemporary Theatre, Macha Monkey Productions, and Fantastic. Z. Other creative outlets include the preparation of copious amounts of coffee and the consumption of any good mystery novel.

Tai Farnsworth is a mixed-race, queer writer based in Los Angeles. She earned her MFA in Creative Writing from Antioch University in 2015. Since then she's been toiling away in education while shopping around her YA manuscript about a girl discovering her bisexuality in the wake of her boyfriend's death. When she's not writing or poisoning young minds with her liberal agenda, she is reading, practicing yoga, and cooking. Her work, which focuses heavily on themes of self-acceptance and queerness, can be found in *Lunch Ticket*, *The Quotable*, *CutBank Literary*, and *The Evansville Review*. She is a 2018 YA mentee through We Need Diverse Books.

Tímea Gulisio is a Hungarian writer, poet, musician, painter and performance artist. Her works are continuously being published both in print and online. Published works: "Nekromantika" (2014), "Baszorkányok" (2014), "A Disznőpásztor" (2015), "Peremvilág" (2015), "Élettársi iszony" (2016), "Vérnarancs" (2017), "Gyásztánc" (2017). Her writings center around the body, liberal approaches, and personal rebellion, and she also employs a great deal of self-irony. Gulisio scrutinizes subordination and superordination in relationships, the intricate world of sexual powerplay, as well as a topic virtually unexplored in modern literature: gerontophilia.

Jade Homa is a passionate dog lover, pasta enthusiast, and sapphic poet. At age 19, she has already written over 120 poems and several short stories. Her poetry covers a variety of topics, from being the girl next door to meeting the girl next door to falling in love with her. Jade narrates the moments of mental illness no one else wants to, the bits even an army of poets couldn't romanticize and spin into something soft. (However, she manages to stay soft, regardless.) Jade currently resides in Allentown, Pennsylvania, and will attend college next year. She is working towards publishing a poetry book in 2019, and is constantly in search of a cute girlfriend.

Sara Koppel started in the Danish Animation industry at the age of fourteen. She simply loved to create hand-drawn animations. In 2002, she was the creator of "Koppel Animation & Naked Love Film." She works around the world on different projects, but most of all she is the maker of more that 20 small independent animation shorts for an adult audience. She has received a lot of awards for work as "Naked Love - Ea's garden" and "Little Vulva & her Clitoral Awareness." She currently is working on a new short film "Embraces & the touch of skin." She also works as an illustrator and artist.

Hannah Larrabee is a poet, science-geek, and former Mainer who grew up on a blueberry farm. Her first full-length collection, Wonder Tissue, won the 2018 Airlie Press Prize. Her chapbook Murmuration (Seven Kitchens Press) is part of the Robin Becker Series for LGBTQ poets. She's had work appear in: The Adirondack Review, Barren Magazine, Harpoon Review, Lambda Literary Spotlight, Rock & Sling, and elsewhere. Hannah was one of 22 artists selected by NASA to see the James Webb Space Telescope, and her JWST poems were displayed at Goddard Space Center. She holds an MFA in Creative Writing from the University of New Hampshire.

Meagan Lyle is a queer artist, organizer and educator who loves exploring the forest, and cooking for family and friends. Painting watercolors brings her internal tranquility and meditative release. A few months ago, she started a project called Beyond Coalescence in an effort to build wider community, share art and send love. It is an opportunity to receive an original watercolor or gift one to someone special. Meagan takes requests once a week, paints them, and sends them off in to mail, often times to strangers. She sends watercolors to folks trapped in the country's awful prison system, folks in detention, folks going through hard times or friends who just want to support her work! She has learned a great deal through this project and hopes to continue growing and improving it.

Lee Lynch is the award-winning author of books including: *Rainbow Gap, The Swashbuckler, Beggar of Love*, and *An American Queer*. Her syndicated column, "The Amazon Trail," has run nationally since 1986. She wrote for "The Ladder." Recently, she co-curated with author Renee Bess *Our Happy Hours, LGBT Voices from the Gay Bars*—proceeds going to GLBT youth organizations. She lives in the Pacific Northwest with her wife, Lainie Lynch and their magnificent cat.

Lynn Martin's poetry has appeared in *Calllope, River City Review, South Florida Review, The Garden State, Green Mountains Review, Sinister Wisdom, Connecticut Review, Earth's Daughters, Sweet Annie Press, The Centennial Review, Chrysalis Reader, Writing Nature, Passager,* and *Friends Journal.* She also has work in the anthologies, *Heartbeat of New England, My Lover Is A woman, Tail Feathers,* and the 2012 anthology, *Connections: N.Y. City bridges in poetry.* Her non-fiction has been published in *The Mystery Review, The Brattleboro Reformer, Out in the Mountains, Foster Families Magazine* and the *Southeastern Audubon Society newsletter.*

Madari Pendàs is a Cuban-American writer and poet living in Miami. Her works focus on the surreal and absurd aspects that accompany living in an exile community, and the inherited identity crisis of being a first generation American. She has received literary awards from Florida International University, in the categories of fiction, poetry, and creative nonfiction. Her works have appeared in the *Accentos Review, The New Tropic, Politicsay,* and *The Miami New Times.*

Sonny Pilling likes to think of herself as a populist poet. Her work has been published in *Embryonic Guernsey*, an anthology put together by the Green Panda Press in Cleveland, and The *GroundUp*, a journal of the radical left based out of New Mexico State University. She has also independently published and distributed 'zines containing her work and the work of other like-minded poets. She's currently working as an assistant editor at *On Spec Magazine*, Canada's longest running speculative fiction magazine, and trying to get a lesbian poetry collective off the ground.

Unpublished since 1984, **lahl sarDyke**'s completed no degrees. Her writing has appeared in living rooms, coffee shops, and various hearts and minds on and off for 40 years, almost as long as she's been out. A prairie loving Dyke, she now lives on Canada's west coast. White, precariously em-bodied, and unable to hold a job for more than a few hours, she tap-danced naked at a lesbian comedy night and once, a friend body-painted her into a tuxedo. A frequent visitor to the bathroom, the streets of Victoria, and her bed, Lahl loves Dykes, community, revolutionaries, roses, talking and walking. Privileged to have a supportive community and to live in a country with socialized medicine and a welfare system, she usually has everything she needs.

Anastazia Schmid is an activist, artist, and graduate independent scholar. She received the Gloria Anzaldúa Award for her work in gender and sexuality by the American Studies Association, and received the Outstanding History Project Award presented by the Indiana Historical Society. Her work and interviews span multimedia sources *including NPR Abolition Journal and Slate Magazine*. Anastazia has presented at national conferences and published works that reveal how gynecology, obstetrics, and American prisons construct and control women. She is co-authoring a book on the same topics soon to be published by The New Press. She is the co-author of the play "The Duchess of Strongtown" currently under production through The Arts Council of Indianapolis and Anna Deavere Smith's "Hidden Hate Hidden Love" series in New York, pending further production.

Sierra Schweitzer is a student at Appalachian State University, pursuing a double major in Studio Art and Multidisciplinary Anthropology. Beginning at the age of eleven she was drawn to photography and has since begun pursuing professional photographic studies. However, during her two years in the arts department at Enloe High School she received a Gold Key Portfolio (2018) awarded by the Scholastics Art and Writing Awards. Although focusing her studies mostly on landscape photography, she has found sexuality an outlet for expressing the importance between the photographer and their subject.

E. M. Sheehan is the pen name of a social sciences academic librarian with several published peer-reviewed research articles under her belt. She also writes historical, LGBT, and women's fiction novels and short stories, which she aspires to publish in the near future. This memoir essay is her first non-academic publication. She is a member of the Women's Fiction Writers Association, and currently lives in Illinois with her son and two cats.

Savannah Slone is a queer writer who is completing her MF. in the Pacific Northwest. Her poetry and short fiction has appeared in or will soon appear in *Glass, Crab Creek Review, FIVE:2:ONE, Pidgeonholes, decomP magazinE, TERSE,* and elsewhere. She serves as the Assistant Poetry Editor for *Boston Accent Lit* and is the Editor-in-Chief of *Homology Lit*. She is the author of *Hearing the Underwater* (Finishing Line Press, 2019). She enjoys reading, knitting, hiking, and discussing intersectional feminism. You can read more of her work at www.savannahslonewriter.com.

Shawn(ta) Smith-Cruz is a zinester, archivist, writer, and black-dyke-participant of community spaces from Brooklyn, NY but trying to figure out where to move next. Personal projects include archiving black lesbian herstorical narratives, memoir writing, and efficiently changing her daughter's diapers. She is a coordinator at the Lesbian Herstory Archives, and an Assistant Professor at the Graduate Center Library, CUNY. Shawn is honored to have co-edited *Sinister Wisdom 103: Celebrating the Michigan Women's Music Festival* and to have contributed to the journal in other issues along the way. She has an MFA in Fiction from Queens College. You can find more on Shawn at https://shawntasmith.commons.gc.cuny.edu/

S. b. Sowbel, born in a city that sits squarely on the Mason-Dixon Line (near the homes of many journals and anthologies that happily publish poetry), has family in North America and South America, work and heart companionship in the cold northeast and the sweltering, central west, and helps adults get college-level credit for learning acquired outside of academic settings.

Mariposa has been a revolutionary since the 1968 police riot at the Democratic National Convention. She has been out as a lesbian since 2015 and has been a feminist since 2017. She majored in women's and gender studies at Queens College in New York City and received her B.A. in 2018. She is a member of a women's liberation group in New York City and a participant in an all women's group at her senior center. She has written three lesbian feminist novels and a book of poetry. She considers herself to be a proud and strong lesbian feminist, dedicated to the destruction of the patriarchy.

Patty Willis' first one-woman play was performed at the Edinburgh Festival Fringe and in Noh theaters in Japan. Her novel about life in the mountain village of Japan where she lived is on the recommended reading list of the Japanese Library Association. In 2010, she wrote, Man from Magdalena, a music theater piece based on a true story from the Arizona borderlands. Performances have funded over $145,000 in micro-loans to Central America and Mexico. In 2014, the Utah Division of Arts and Museums awarded her a prize in creative non-fiction for "Dancing Bird's Apprentice," a work imagined from the diaries of her Mormon pioneer ancestor Patty Bartlett Sessions and now a play Midwife. She is the recipient of the Bailey Prize for literature. Her poems have been published in Sunstone and will be published in *Sinister Wisdom* this year. After serving a Unitarian Universalist congregation in Salt Lake City for six years, she and her wife have recently settled in the Washington, D.C. area where she is enjoying a sabbatical year of writing.

Sarah Yasuda is a writer and translator based in Boston, Massachusetts. She is currently an MLIS candidate at Simmons College, concentrating on Cultural Heritage Informatics. Prior to Boston, she lived and worked in Tokyo as an educator and translator. Her short stories focus on gender identity, women, and the Asian American experience. She is currently working on a novel about anxious women morphing into food. Check out more of her short stories, book reviews, and thoughts on her blog at emptysignified.wordpress.com.

Lynette Yetter envisions an egalitarian world where we all live together in harmony with Mother Nature. She is a graduate student in the Master of Arts in Liberal Studies program at Reed College in Portland, Oregon. Her poetry was nominated for a Pushcart Prize. She played panpipes on the Academy Award nominated documentary *Recycled Life*. She authored the novel *Lucy Plays Panpipes for Peace* and the creative nonfiction book *72 Money Saving Tips for the 99%*. Lynette makes music, movies, books and art to touch your soul and make you think. You can check out her work at www.LynetteYetter.com.

SHARING OUR LESBIAN HERSTORY: *SINISTER WISDOM* BACK ISSUES

For the past forty-two years, *Sinister Wisdom* has documented lesbian history in the pages of the journal. Now with over 100 issues in circulation, the journal has an impressive back list and tens of thousands of copies are in circulation. Over the past year and for the next year or two, *Sinister Wisdom* is working to ensure that all of our back issues find homes with appreciative lesbian readers. We would love for you to help us in this work.

In December 2016, *Sinister Wisdom* editor and publisher moved the over 9,000 copies of back issues from a storage facility in Berkeley, California to her home office in Dover, Florida. While that seemed like a monumental task, the real work began when the issues arrived: distributing them throughout the world to people interested in reading and cherishing lesbians's words. The goal is to have all 9,000 copies of these issues out of the Dover offices by the end of 2018. Will you join us and help distribute the journal's back issues?

Here is our plan for distribution:

- <u>Individual copies are available for purchase</u>. The *Sinister Wisdom* website is complete up-to-date and people can order back issues online. The first fifty-seven issues are also available as PDF downloads to anyone interested.
- *Sinister Wisdom* is free on request to women in prisons and psychiatric institutions. Back issues can also be requested by women and shipped to these locations. *Sinister Wisdom*'s goal is to communicate to these women that they are not alone and are a part of a larger community that supports them.

- All available back issues are available for only the cost of shipping ($20) to LGBT centers, women's resource centers, and other community centers that provide support and resources for lesbian communities. A set of all available back issues of *Sinister Wisdom* is free upon request to community centers who wish to provide *Sinister Wisdom* as a resource.
- Teach *Sinister Wisdom*! Teaching guides are available for these issues of *Sinister Wisdom*: *Sinister Wisdom* 32: *Special Issue on Death, Healing, Mourning, and Illness* (Summer 1987), *Sinister Wisdom* 36: *Surviving Psychiatric Assault & Creating Emotional Well-Being in Our Communities* (Winter 1988/89), *Sinister Wisdom* 43/44: *The 15th Anniversary Retrospective* (Summer 1991), *Sinister Wisdom* 47: *Tellin' It Like It Tis'* (Summer/Fall 1992), *Sinister Wisdom* 48: *Lesbian Resistance* (Winter 1992/93), *Sinister Wisdom* 49: *The Lesbian Body* (Spring/Summer 1993), *Sinister Wisdom* 50: *The Ethics Issue... Not!* (Summer/Fall 1993), *Sinister Wisdom* 51 (Winter 1993/94), *Sinister Wisdom* 54: *Lesbians and Religion: Questions of Faith and Community* (Winter 1994/95), and *Sinister Wisdom* 58: *Open Issue* (Winter/Spring 1998).
- Instructors who adopt any of these issues can receive for only the cost of shipping enough copies of the journal for each and every student in the class. (The Women's Movement is generous and wants young people to have books of their own!)
- *Sinister Wisdom* documents lesbian historical issues often missed in history books. *Sinister Wisdom*'s back issues come with full teaching guides that contain the historical background, key concepts, discussion questions, teaching activities, and a breakdown of what is in the issue. A full teaching set of an issue is free upon

request to professors and universities interested in teaching an issue(s) of the journal.
- Read *Sinister Wisdom* with your book group! Back issues, paired with discussion/teaching guides, are perfect for reading groups that want to explore lesbian literature and art that chronicle lesbian history over the past forty-one years. Issues of *Sinister Wisdom* stand alone, but they can also be used as introductions to readings of the notable contributors whose work have been published in *Sinister Wisdom* such as Adrienne Rich, Audre Lorde, tatiana de la tierra, Minnie Bruce Pratt, Pat Parker, Elana Dykewomon, and others. Select copies are available free for book groups interested in reading them. Check out the Sinister Wisdom website for more information: www.sinisterwisdom.org/bookgroups
- *Sinister Wisdom* actively places collections of the journals with institutional archives and community archives. If you know of a local archive without a run of *Sinister Wisdom*, put us in touch so that we can preserve the journal for people to read and enjoy.
- *Sinister Wisdom* would also be delighted to send back issues of the journal to any other spaces that celebrate lesbian art and culture. Reach out to us; we are happy to ship back issues.

For interested groups or individuals, contact Julie R. Enszer, editor of *Sinister Wisdom*, at julie@sinisterwisdom.org. Find a list of back issues at sinisterwisdom.org/issues.

If you have back issues of the journal that you no longer want, first look to see if there is a local organization or archive that would like to have an maintain copies. If you cannot find a great home close to you, please feel free to send copies to us and we redistribute them. Send them to us at 2333 McIntosh Rd. Dover, FL 33527.

THANK YOU TO VOLUNTEERS, INTERNS, AND BOOKSELLERS

Sinister Wisdom appreciates the time and energy of volunteers and student interns in helping to keep the magazine running and vibrant. Thank you to:

Sara Gregory for all her work this spring and summer on the journal and the calendar (congratulations on the new job!)

Sophia Moore, summer intern from University of California Berkeley who worked on this issue and research support to *Sinister Wisdom*'s editor and publisher

Talia Sieff, summer and fall intern from University of Maryland who worked on a forthcoming Sapphic Classic and is rocking our Facebook page

Cassandra Johnson, volunteer and mail guru in Florida

2018 Guest Editors: J.P. Howard, Amber Atiya, Sara Gregory, Olga Garcia, Maylei Blackwell, Barbara Esrig, Merril Mushroom, Rose Norman, Cheryl Clarke, Morgan Gwenwald, Stevie Jones, & Red Washburn

The many, many volunteers who organized amazing events all year in local communities.

Members of the *Sinister Wisdom* Board of Directors.

Thank you to everyone who helps *Sinister Wisdom* in so many ways every single day.

Booksellers Carrying *Sinister Wisdom* This Year
Antigone Books - Tucson AZ
Artbook @ MoMAPS1 - Long Island City NY
Bookwoman Bookstore - Austin TX
Bureau of General Services Queer Division The Center - NYC
Charis Books - Atlanta GA
Dog Eared Books - San Francisco CA
Feelmore - Oakland CA

L'Euguélionne Librairie Féministe – Montreal QC
Lighthouse - Edinburgh's Radical Bookshop - Edinburgh Scotland UK
Quimby's Bookstore - Brooklyn NY
Quimby's Bookstore - Chicago IL
Room of One's Own - Madison WI
Schomburg Shop - New York NY
Skylight Books - Los Angeles CA
Talking Leaves Bookstore - Buffalo NY
Violet Valley Bookstore - Water Valley MS
Women & Children First – Chicago IL

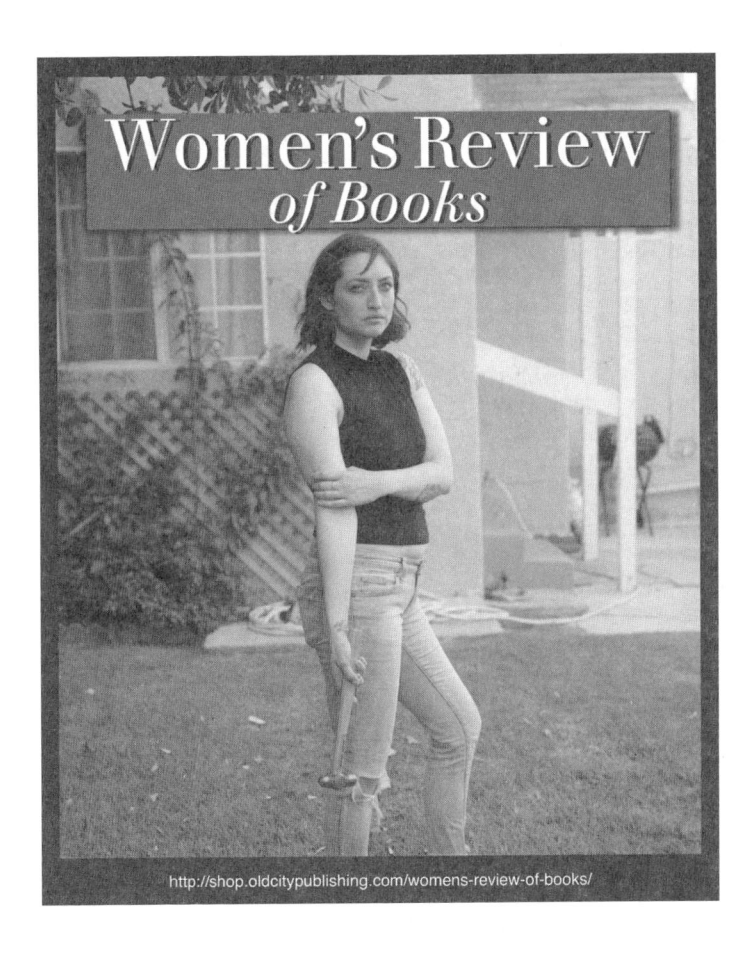

Women's Review of Books

http://shop.oldcitypublishing.com/womens-review-of-books/

Sinister Wisdom **Back Issues Available**

- 110 Legacies of Resistance: Dump Trump ($14)
- 109 Hot Spots: Creating Lesbian Space in the South ($14)
- 108 For The Hard Ones. Para las duras ($18.95)
- 107 Black Lesbians— We Are the Revolution! ($14)
- 104 Lesbianima Rising: Lesbian-Feminist Arts in the South, 1974–96 ($12)
- 103 Celebrating the Michigan Womyn's Music Festival ($12)
- 102 The Complete Works of Pat Parker ($22.95)
- 98 Landykes of the South ($12)
- 97 Out Latina Lesbians ($12)
- 96 What Can I Ask ($18.95)
- 93 Southern Lesbian-Feminist Herstory 1968–94 ($12)
- 91 Living as a Lesbian ($17.95)
- 88 Crime Against Nature ($17.95)
- 84 Time/Space
- 83 Identity and Desire
- 82 In Amerika They Call Us Dykes: Lesbian Lives in the 70s
- 81 Lesbian Poetry – When? And Now!
- 80 Willing Up and Keeling Over
- 78/79 Old Lesbians/Dykes II
- 77 Environmental Issues Lesbian Concerns
- 76 Open Issue
- 75 Lesbian Theories/Lesbian Controversies
- 73 The Art Issue
- 71 Open Issue
- 70 30th Anniversary Celebration
- 67 Lesbians and Work
- 65 Lesbian Mothers & Grandmothers
- 63 Lesbians and Nature
- 58 Open Issue
- 57 Healing
- 54 Lesbians & Religion
- 53 Old Dykes/Lesbians – Guest Edited by Lesbians Over 60
- 52 Allies Issue
- 51 New Lesbian Writing
- 50 Not the Ethics Issue
- 49 The Lesbian Body
- 48 Lesbian Resistance Including work by Dykes in Prison
- 47 Lesbians of Color: Tellin' It Like It 'Tis
- 46 Dyke Lives
- 45 Lesbians & Class (the first issue of a lesbian journal edited entirely by poverty and working class dykes)
- 43/44 15th Anniversary double-size (368 pgs) retrospective
- 39 Disability
- 36 Surviving Psychiatric Assault/ Creating emotional well being
- 34 Sci-Fi, Fantasy & Lesbian Visions
- 33 Wisdom
- 32 Open Issue

Back issues are $6.00 unless noted plus $3.00 Shipping & Handling for 1st issue; $1.00 for each additional issue. Order online at www.sinisterwisdom.org

Or mail check or money order to:
Sinister Wisdom
2333 McIntosh Road
Dover, FL 33527-5980